Nicole Haddow is a journalist and author of *Smashed Avocado: How I Cracked the Property Market and You Can Too* and *The Ethical Investor.* She has written for *The Age*, *Sydney Morning Herald*, *The Guardian*, *Australian Financial Review*, *Domain*, *Madison*, *Cleo* and more. She lives in regional Victoria with her husband, Sam, and fur girls Frankie and Olive, and is working on several projects while they renovate their heritage home together.

NICOLE HADDOW

BUILDING A STRONG FINANCIAL FUTURE AND AN EVEN BETTER RELATIONSHIP

hachette
AUSTRALIA

hachette AUSTRALIA

Published in Australia and New Zealand in 2023
by Hachette Australia
(an imprint of Hachette Australia Pty Limited)
Gadigal Country, Level 17, 207 Kent Street, Sydney, NSW 2000
www.hachette.com.au

Hachette Australia acknowledges and pays our respects to the past, present and future Traditional Owners and Custodians of Country throughout Australia and recognises the continuation of cultural, spiritual and educational practices of Aboriginal and Torres Strait Islander peoples. Our head office is located on the lands of the Gadigal people of the Eora Nation.

A catalogue record for this work is available from the National Library of Australia

ISBN: 978 0 7336 5040 6 (paperback)

Cover and illustration design by Adam Williams
Author photograph by Melissa Decarli
Typeset in 11.5/18pt Adobe Caslon Pro by Kirby Jones
Printed and bound in Australia by McPherson's Printing Group

The paper this book is printed on is certified against the Forest Stewardship Council® Standards. McPherson's Printing Group holds FSC® chain of custody certification SA-COC-005379. FSC® promotes environmentally responsible, socially beneficial and economically viable management of the world's forests.

For Sam,

who makes each day a way of life

Contents

Introduction

A quiet, reflective moment in May 2022 would be the beginning of the end of my life as I'd known it. It'd been exactly a year since I'd packed up my stuff and moved into my historic, dilapidated home. The long-held dream of owning a freestanding cottage had been my motivation. Making it a reality on a single income meant moving ninety minutes from Melbourne to the regional town of Ballarat where I knew no one. The Victorian weatherboard, built circa 1910, was in desperate need of love. Sure, I'd never renovated before, but how hard could it be? Quite hard, it transpires.

I spent hundreds of hours up and down a ladder, patching crumbling plaster and painting rooms. I lifted kitchen floor tiles with the help of family and friends. I upcycled the old floral carpet, turning it into a hallway runner and circle rug. I lacquered cheap timber that became temporary benchtops until I could afford a proper kitchen renovation. It was a challenge, but I relished it, even if it often felt like I'd bitten off more than I could chew.

On that autumn evening, the first anniversary of my arrival, I sipped a glass of wine, gazed out the window of my half-renovated house and sat with a conflicting swirl of feelings. I knew I'd made these choices consciously, and yet I'd never expected to spend the final year of my thirties living alone in a rickety regional dwelling. While getting to this point was something that I was proud to have achieved – I was gathering a stack of handy skills and the house was slowly becoming the home I'd imagined – it had also been a long and lonely slog. I wondered if things could, or *should*, be different.

Could I have played my cards more effectively? Was I insane to have held out for a great love? I hadn't meant to, but even though shouldering a huge financial burden on my own was daunting, I'd become uncomfortable with the idea of someone else having a say in my finances. Perhaps subconsciously I'd stayed single so that if anyone was to blame for a possible fiscal failure, it'd be me and me alone. I did, however, like the idea of having a companion. A partner; an equal. Such a person had so far been elusive.

I hadn't done myself many favours moving to a regional town, where it seemed everyone within a suitable age bracket was already coupled up, and the number of eligible blokes was extremely limited. An occasional flick through the dating apps was usually over fast. I'd swipe a handful of options in my radius before I landed on a screen saying I'd run out of possible matches in my area.

Continuing to put energy into the digital pursuit of love seemed pointless. And yet, as I drained my wine glass and began to shuffle random items from the fridge into some form of dinner, I decided to give it one last go, this time with a far more open mind.

When I saw Sam's face, I thought he was handsome, but he was also younger than me. Still, he looked like fun. I swiped right and treated it as an opportunity to meet a new and interesting person. He didn't have to be 'the one'.

Soon after we matched, we arranged to meet for a drink at a wine bar. The conversation was slow and cautious to begin with. Halfway through our second drink, he said something incredibly witty, and I thought, *Oh, I like this guy.*

At the end of the evening, Sam walked me to my car, which I'd happened to park right next to his ute. As we prepared to say goodbye, the lightest misty rain started falling and glowed orange, backlit by a street lamp. A couple argued in the background while we hovered nervously. An uncertain embrace led to the kiss that changed everything.

Our second date went for most of the weekend. By the end of our third date, I had a key to his place, and we'd discussed moving in together. For weeks I wandered around like a dazed, heart-eyed emoji. I'd never felt like this before. We were absolutely head over heels for each other.

Under ordinary circumstances, couples have more time to build their bond before they whip out a budgeting spreadsheet and open a joint bank account, but Sam's property lease was coming to an end. We knew we wanted to be together, and as a landscaper with several construction skills, he was both willing and excited to help me bring the house to life. 'My gut is telling me to dive right in,' he told me.

I had the same instinct – not a doubt in my mind that I'd met my match. But our differing financial positions did have the potential to create tension. Sam was upfront, telling me that he had a bit of debt. By contrast, I had a home. I had worked so hard to secure a property on my own, and I'd always been fierce when it came to telling other women to protect their assets. Yet, I had no idea how to actually do the right thing for myself, without compromising the wonderful early stages of our romance.

Sam told me to do whatever made me feel comfortable – that he'd sign anything that cemented my rights.

If we were going to be together long-term, I wanted him to clear his debt first. So instead of paying rent, he spent the first few months reducing the amount owing on a personal loan. But in lieu of cash towards the mortgage, he contributed to the house in ways that improved it and added value. In the first week, he fixed the shed roof, something that probably would have cost me $500 if

I'd hired a handyman. Next, he sourced old Baltic pine floorboards to fix a considerable hole in the bedroom floor that, up until that point, I'd covered with cardboard and magazines. Then we started painting together.

It wasn't all work, though. Sam regularly crafted cocktails on cold nights and transported us to Hawaii with his record collection and mood lighting. Watching our spending didn't mean forgoing the romance.

We spent weekends walking around the house working out what was needed in each room and the order in which to do things. Sam called trades for things we didn't want to do ourselves, such as sanding and polishing the old floors. He arranged the quotes and booked the jobs in. These were things that I could have done but sharing the mental load of the project was a huge weight lifted. Our vision for the property crystalised; our connection grew deeper.

That said, I had to decide what was reasonable to ask of him if things went wrong. Of course we scoffed, 'Won't happen to us!' But I had to know we agreed on a fair outcome if we did split up.

Here's where I landed:

We'd establish what the property was worth at the point the relationship came to an end, and I'd be entitled to everything that I'd put in before he arrived, then we'd split any remaining profits 50/50. It could potentially mean refinancing the property to give Sam his share; it could also mean selling.

Writing that down makes me feel sick. Saying it out loud was difficult, but it had to be done.

Prior to settling on that arrangement, I did a bit of research, and I was stunned to find how little information there is available to people entering relationships and merging finances. We've well and truly moved on from the housewife era. Most relationships are dual income and many people have put careers before family, or they've re-entered relationships after separations. Often, when we do find someone to settle down with, each half of the pair is going to be bringing stuff they are within their right to protect.

What's a fair split of expenses when one person earns more than the other? Should everything go in a joint bank account? At what point should your partner be listed on the mortgage? What are the tax implications?

But, most importantly: how do you manage money in a way that helps you work towards goals, empowers both of the individuals in the relationship and keeps the love story going too?

In my first book, *Smashed Avocado*, I charted my path to home ownership, while in *The Ethical Investor*, I explored ways I could diversify my investments beyond housing, thinking about everything from superannuation to shares, all while seeking investments that were good for society and our planet.

I had been so caught up in personal finance that I hadn't seriously considered what it means to manage money as a couple or family. On the surface it can be easy to maintain a level of autonomy initially, which is what Sam and I did: separate bank accounts, an agreement about who paid for what and a joint savings account.

But I felt that keeping all finances separate was to keep each other at arm's length emotionally. I'm certain our relationship would be far less fulfilling if I'd told Sam that he could move in and pay rent at *my* house. The day he moved in, the house became *ours*. It had to, because it's not just where we live, the restoration is a shared project that we're working on together. I suspected this would be the key to our success: equal ownership of the vision, both short and long-term.

This made me realise that some couples might get so focused on the dollars, cents and day-to-day equality of their relationship that they're not looking up from the budget to the road ahead. Are you going in the same direction? Where are you a year from now? A decade? Sure, the goal posts move over time, but if one person wants to quit their job and live off-grid, while the other is saving for a waterfront mansion, there's going to be issues at some point, no matter how much you love each other.

That said, I understand why many people focus on their own funds and splitting the cost of living equitably. If you're anything like me, this mashed-up era of feminism, rom-coms, girl power and personal-finance influencers has you wildly confused about how to balance your own aspirations with being a great partner.

So, in this book I have attempted to clear up this modern mess. I've asked couples questions that I definitely wouldn't ask at a dinner party. I've found out how successful pairs are building wealth together and I've investigated whether there's a correlation between great relationships and financial freedom.

But, before we kick off, it's important to know there's no one right way to manage your money as a couple. Your goals, lifestyle and current financial circumstances will be different to ours. The aim of this book is not to give you a strict set of rules, but to give you a peek inside the lives of other couples and a seat at the table with experts you mightn't otherwise have access to, so that you can expand your shared worldview, get aligned and perhaps dream bigger as a team than you have in the past.

In the coming chapters, you'll hear from qualified professionals. I'm approaching everything as one half of a couple who was curious to know if there was an optimal way to manage our money together, so I've consulted with financial planners, lawyers, accountants and tax experts, and their advice is general in nature. It won't apply precisely to you and your circumstances as a couple. If it does get you thinking about what you'd like to achieve together, it's best to speak to a licensed professional before making decisions about where you want to go from here.

With help from these experts, I've compiled a range of hints, tips and guidance to help you to make better money decisions as a team. Hopefully, it'll help all of us smash our couple goals.

Finally, this book is not strictly about money, it's about how the quality of your relationship can help or hinder your ability to achieve your goals. Interestingly, whether I was speaking to financial experts or relationship therapists, there was one common piece of advice. It is essential to have tough conversations, and have them regularly, so at the end of each chapter, I'll give you questions to ask one another based on what we've covered. With honest and transparent communication, I'm certain you'll be setting and beginning to achieve your couple goals in no time.

Okay, let's get stuck into it!

CHAPTER ONE

A quick chat about financial inequality

Anecdotally, I know establishing a money-management strategy as a couple can be a messy exercise. I've asked many couples if their shared financial processes came easily and the overwhelming response was 'No, it was so hard!' That's because anyone who came of age after the 1990s is setting a precedent for relationships and the way that income is handled as a pair. In fact, dual income couples managing their finances in innovative ways are pretty much pioneers.

Looking back to school yards of the 1980s and 1990s, families were still overwhelmingly nuclear, most often with two heterosexual parents. If you were getting picked up from school, chances were that it was Mum who was standing at the gate. My family was pretty stock standard. For the most part, Dad was the breadwinner and Mum worked 'part-time'. I put part-time in quote marks because honestly the shit that she did in a day was all work, every hour of it: breakfast, making school lunches, school drop-off, actual paid employment, school pick-up, after-school appointments, dinner, the bedtime routine and preparing for the next day. It was a relentless, demanding and largely thankless full-time role. It just wasn't accurately reflected in the household accounting.

I had assumed that my millennial generation experienced the last of that. With women getting into the workforce in increasing numbers from the 1960s, you'd think by the early 2000s, full-time dual income couples would well and truly replace a male breadwinner.

And yet in 2016 – *yes, 2016!* – the *Sydney Morning Herald* reported:

> Australia has a very high ratio of part-time work compared with its peers and women hold nearly three-quarters of all those jobs. That's helped create the 1.5 worker household – with a full-time dad and part-time mum – which has become one of the bedrocks of modern Australia.

Don't even get me started on how traditionally gendered that quote is.

I did a bit of digging to better understand that the foundation of this 'bedrock of modern Australia' was laid in 1907. This was the year of the Harvester Decision, made by Justice Higgins. In a case before him, a bunch of workers from the Sunshine Harvester Factory in Melbourne were getting paid differently for the same work – some 6 shillings a day, others 5 – and they wanted equality; also, they wanted enough to actually live on.

Justice Higgins reckoned that 7 shillings a day – 42 shillings a week – seemed like a fair sum for an unskilled labourer to take home and support a wife and three kids. By the 1920s, the precedent had made way for Australia's 'basic wage' – essentially the minimum wage we have today.

It was certainly a historic decision that set income standards. Problem was, it also set us up for the gender pay gap we're still battling to close. In 1912, Justice Higgins was back in the decision-making chair at the Court of Arbitration dealing with the Fruit Pickers Case. In this instance, he thought that women should be paid the same as men, but only if they did male-dominant jobs ...

Eventually, we ended up with centralised wage fixing, through which the basic wage for males was set much higher than it was for women. I guess it just made more financial sense for Dad to go out and get on the tools, and for Mum to do absolutely everything else in the household for little to no income.

Obviously, that wasn't a fair or ideal scenario for couples or their relationships. It has also given us a bleak history of women having a reduced say in how household financial decisions were made. Is it any wonder that marriages began to fail in greater and greater numbers?

It took until 1969 for equal pay for equal work to be recognised in the courts, but it was still a slog from there. And we're still slogging. In 2022, the national gender pay gap was 14.1 per cent, or about $263.90 a week in favour of males, but by mid-2023, the gap was down to 13 per cent and has been closing steadily in the past decade.

One approach to addressing the gender pay gap is the Workplace Gender Equity Amendment (Closing the Gender Pay Gap) Bill, which was passed in March 2023. The reform allowed the Workplace Gender Equality Agency (WGEA) to publish gender pay gaps of private organisations with more than 100 employees from 2024, with public sector data to follow. But there was no plan for repercussions for those who are found to contribute to the gender pay gap.

Also, these reports will inevitably be flawed. A 2023 article in *The Conversation* reported that summaries don't provide a reliable snapshot of individual scenarios. The author pointed out that in a company where everyone is paid equally, but the CEO is paid ten times more, the company would be seen to have a 17.6 per cent pay gap. Contrast that with a tech company, where every woman is paid 2 per cent less than every man, but the founder doesn't take a salary: 'The aggregate numbers will show no gender pay gap.'

That said, the financial composition of our households is changing dramatically. According to the 2021 census, there were more than 5.5 million couples, 53 per cent of which had kids living with them and 47 per cent who didn't have kids at home. There were more than a million one-parent families. And, with the exception of the close to 25,000 same-sex marriages recorded, this data doesn't account for relationships across the entire LGBTIQA+ community.

In addition, while the gender pay gap remains, some women are either out-earning their partners, or coming to the relationship with an asset they've secured solo. Although women required a male guarantor to take out a loan in Australia up until the 1970s, they're definitely making up for lost time, with millennial women now among the fastest growing cohorts of homebuyers.

The combination of a gender pay gap and a rise in women snapping up homes on their own might be confusing, but the point is that there are so many different financial dynamics at play, it can be incredibly difficult to navigate the countless scenarios.

The gender pay gap is only one part of the overall challenge for women who want to work full-time for the length of their careers. The figures that show women buying property in higher numbers than men don't account for the nuances of life after the initial purchase. If you plan to have children, and also have breasts, you may intend to use your body as a source of food for your tiny offspring, there's still a broad expectation that you stay at home, or at least out of the workplace, while you do so. The question becomes, how long will you stay home? How will your housing costs be covered during that time? Will Dad step up to the parenting plate if you want to return to your career? Statistically speaking, he probably won't take on the kids in a full-time capacity, with the number of Australian stay-at-home dads still hovering around the staggeringly low 5 per cent mark. On balance, to be fair to the blokes, we still have systemic societal conditions that have set up stay-at-home parenting and primary caregiving to be a female-driven operation, regardless of whether the woman works or not. As Annabel Crabb pointed out in her 2019 essay 'Men at Work', 'When a woman has a baby, our society and the vast majority of workplaces are geared to expect – accurately, by and large – that she will be primarily responsible for the care and supervision of that baby. When that baby gets sick, it is she who will stay home from work.' The physical ability to go out and earn is only one factor in any couple's pursuit of both wealth and contentment. It's the overall loss of income, career progression and satisfaction that potentially hits both people at various times, but more often women will fare worse, especially if the relationship ends in the years or decades after children come along. With a prolonged gap on a CV, they may never excel to a position they could have if they'd climbed to senior roles without children tugging at their feet from below. And yet the Australian gender earnings gap research also points to findings from other countries, such as Norway, which have showed the financial penalty that came with having a child was much larger for women in heterosexual couples than it was for same-sex couples.

That shows us that the income loss that comes with parenthood shouldn't solely be the cost of the person who gives birth. I so often hear that it makes no sense financially for a woman to go back to work due to the cost of childcare. Why is this a mother's burden to shoulder? Childcare is a family cost, it's not Mum's job to bankroll it. If you are a dual income couple, it may be time to start looking at your collective income and your wealth-building power as a team. The costs associated with life as a committed couple, whether you have children or not, are the responsibility of both people. In the coming chapters we'll explore ways to shift your mindset regarding gender-based financial roles in case that's a challenge you face in your relationship.

Even if you don't take the family path, you may experience other forms of financial inequality. For example, at times, one of you may be unable to work due to accident or illness, one party may choose to take a pay cut to pursue a long-held dream or someone needs to make professional sacrifices to care for an aging parent or sick family member. Maximising income, supporting family and nurturing career identity is a *couple's* shared duty. You need to talk about these realities as a united team sooner rather than later if you're going to successfully tackle them together without either of you being professionally or financially penalised in the long run.

Couple goals check-in

In the coming chapters, I'll give you heaps of talking points that will hopefully help you to refine your views on money, your relationship and your goals. I'm not going to kick off here by asking you to delve deeply into your views on financial inequality and the gender pay gap. But I will ask you to pause for a moment and think about what was modelled to you growing up and how that might affect your partner. This will help you prepare for our next challenge: talking about money together.

- What was the financial dynamic like in your household growing up?
- Did both of your parents work?
- Were you in a single-parent family? If so, how did that parent juggle work and family?
- Did one of your parents experience a financial penalty for staying home to raise you?
- How have these experiences shaped your own attitude towards financial equality in relationships?

CHAPTER TWO

Early days: how to talk about money without killing the spark

Let's lighten the mood for a second. If you've just met someone and you're gushing all over the place, you're, understandably, not likely to be obsessing about the broad impact of the social and gender inequality we've just discussed. If you're anything like me you're regularly uttering the word *finally*. You've made it Instagram official, met their mates and you're listening to a lot of 80s power ballads (okay, maybe that particular example only applies to me). It's a damn fine feeling. No games, no red flags, just glorious green ones flapping in the breeze, marking the starting line on your shared path. That's probably the biggest green flag of them all: looking to the future together. Chances are that you as an individual have some ideas about what you want your future to look like: you have hopes and dreams. And it's likely that you're going to need money to set up the life you desire. Similarly, your partner will have their own concept of what the days and years ahead could hold.

That means you're going to have to talk about how you'll fund your life together. But how do you talk about money without killing the spark in your new relationship? In the early days of dating, you might not feel comfortable laying out your spending habits but early conversations about money are crucial to setting up a healthy, happy relationship – and a healthy bank balance later on. Most people aren't taught to have these conversations in a productive, respectful way. There's so much more to having meaningful, intimate chats than simply divulging everything that's on your mind and assuming that will be met with a positive response.

I'm really comfortable talking about money. But it's something I've had to work on. In the past, I have dismissed and avoided conversations about money, mostly because I hadn't wanted to expose my shortcomings. Fake it till you make it and all that. Most people don't go around announcing how much debt they're in or celebrating how much they regret past spending.

Bad money habits often shine a spotlight on our flaws, weaknesses, vices and vulnerability. If we're not happy with our current financial position or our habits, we have to confront ourselves. I have upped my credit card limits instead of addressing my shitty behaviour with money more times than I care to admit. For me, turning around my financial position meant accepting that in my twenties I'd been funding a lifestyle well beyond my earning capacity. That I'd been lying to myself. That getting ahead was going to mean sacrifice and living within my means (well below my means for a while at first, actually).

I've had some very difficult conversations with myself in recent years and making lasting changes took a long time. I know there are still areas I can improve – I'm human after all. It was acceptable to go at my own pace when I was on my own because there was no one else to be accountable to, or for. Had someone asked me to change faster, they would have met with resistance. So, with all this said, I know that beginning a discussion about money must be handled delicately.

If you know you need to make big changes to achieve your goals, the first step is simply to start talking openly and honestly, knowing that there's no magic overnight fix, and that each individual will need to go at their own pace.

The upside of initiating conversations about your financial situation is that it can be incredibly intimate when done well. Intimacy – a feeling of closeness and emotional connection – requires both of you to bring deep thoughts and feelings into your relationship. You need to be prepared to drop your guard and be vulnerable. Doing this helps the other person understand you even better than they did before. It requires trust and support. When you do this from a financial perspective, you're likely sharing experiences of your own relationship with money, along with your childhood and family experiences with spending and saving, as this will have shaped your present behaviour to an extent. You're also revealing failures from the past, fears, shame and hopes for the future. It's a *lot*.

I knew this based on my own experience of having tough money chats, but I've never been formally taught how to have productive conversations that generate positive outcomes, especially with a partner. So, I consulted couples' therapist and sexologist Isiah McKimmie to learn what she teaches her clients.

As I'd already suspected, Isiah confirms, 'Couples who talk well about issues around money are more likely to stay together. We know that supportive relationships have huge benefits in other areas of their lives.'

Before you begin a serious discussion about your financial life together, it's worth considering some skills that successful couples have. The first is called 'accepting influence' which essentially means being able to see and respect your partner's perspective, opinions and feelings. Ultimately, it means there's not one person running the show, you're both influencing the way in which you work towards your goals.

The second key skill is compromise. If you're out to 'win' or get your way without being prepared to find common ground, you're not practising the skill of accepting influence.

Hopefully you have those skills, or you're prepared to work on them, because money conversations not only bring up a lot of emotions, they can potentially surface the two emotions that can do the most damage in a relationship: fear and shame. Shame associated with money is a considerable hurdle because it's a strong internal noose. At its worst, it can cause us to bury our heads in the sand, freeze up and avoid taking positive steps forward.

But it's like strengthening a muscle – the more you do it, the better you'll get. Once you've both considered your ability to accept influence, compromise and understand that financial matters are closely linked to strong emotional responses, it's time to think about the dynamics in your relationship. This is not just about the subject you're debating but rather *how* you conduct your discussion. For instance, have a think about whether one person does all the talking. Are you both sharing your aspirations, concerns and flaws equally?

Often, Isiah's clients will tell her they've had a conversation, but in reality they haven't actually listened to each other. By contrast, in conversations that are fruitful, both people feel like they can share openly and be properly understood.

Success in financial intimacy requires reinforcement of your love and commitment to one another, especially when there's a lot of vulnerability on display. If revealing your financial self is met with true listening, support and respect, you'll likely feel a stronger bond than you did before.

According to Isiah, the sooner you talk about money, the better. Often couples who talk about money early 'are more successful than couples who don't'. You might still be feeling nervous about discussing numbers so you'll probably be relieved to hear that in the early stages of a relationship there are ways to build up your intimate conversational skills without leaping to spreadsheets and wealth projections. The best way to start is by understanding each other's values, life goals and what's important to your partner. Ask them questions: how do they want their working week to play out, where do they envisage living and how do they see their life going forward?

It's really not the subject of money or the specific questions that matter, Isiah explains, but *how* couples talk about issues and how open they are to each other's perspective that makes the difference.

Early money discussions

Here are a few discussion topics to help you open up to each other about your past, present and future.

Money in childhood

Revealing aspects of your early family life might help you find some empathy if you struggle with the way your partner manages money. Some people follow in their parents' footsteps, others take a polar-opposite direction. Maybe you've watched your folks behave recklessly with money and as a result you're now incredibly conservative. Maybe your partner's childhood was extremely disadvantaged and so they save everything they can. Perhaps they were really fortunate and have always been able to buy what they've wanted or needed, but that might also mean they're not great with a budget. Sharing this information might also help you establish common ground if you've experienced anything similar. Importantly, it enables you to see what childhood experiences they bring to the person they are today.

Spending habits

Conscious and unconscious behaviour associated with spending is closely tied to values, which aren't static, so habits and priorities may have changed over the course of your partner's life. I used to love spending money on clothes because great outfits made me feel good about myself. I still like to have quality clothes, but I don't spend nearly as much as I once did because I want more to show for my days than a wardrobe full of stuff. Today I prefer to spend money on experiences, weekends away and nice meals. Sam loves nothing more than trawling for second-hand vinyl as music is one of his greatest passions. Building his record collection is something I'd never want to take away from him. Our shared splurges are something we can both enjoy – a weekend away and maybe a few records collected on our travels is always a win. We don't begrudge one another's spending in these areas as long as it fits within our budget.

Spending, saving and investing approaches

This might be a good topic to discuss before you try to set up a savings plan together so you know what you're in for in terms of enthusiasm or resistance. It'll help you to understand whether they lived within their means prior to your relationship and perhaps give you more of an insight into their financial position if you're not ready to ask about what they do or don't have straight-up. It's far less confrontational than asking how much they have saved and whether they have any debt.

Aspirations

Sharing aspirations will give you a sense of what they'd like to work towards and whether that's something you want too. Maybe they want a house or a farm. Perhaps they'd like to be a digital nomad or work for a charity in a developing nation, in which case you'll want to ask yourself if your own ambitions are a fit in that scenario. Their answers mightn't be blatantly financial. When I talked about this with Sam, he told me that 'success is coming home to a warm bowl of minestrone'. In other words, he's grateful for simple pleasures. As long as he has good food and quality companionship, he's pretty damn happy.

He doesn't aspire to a demanding all-encompassing job because he doesn't need an extravagant lifestyle. In choosing Sam, I know I have a partner who takes a holistic approach to success and places a great deal of importance on the success of our relationship and the fulfilment we give each other every day. Prior to meeting him, professional success was a big driver for me, and he's brought far more balance to my view of what constitutes a good life. We're very happy living a quiet life in our country cottage, but if I had a burning desire to be a CEO and wanted to work around the clock to achieve that, I know the quality of our relationship would erode over time. That's not to say I don't have ambitions anymore, because I do and I continue to pursue them, but I don't have professional goals that are wildly misaligned with our lifestyle or commitment to our relationship.

Tips for successful money talks

Talking about money becomes increasingly natural with frequency. Once you've nailed your ability to talk about broad financial topics, you can start to talk about how money works for you as a pair.

This may or may not align with moving in together, but for the purpose of this exercise, let's say you're planning to talk about the foundation of your couple goals. You need to have a transparent discussion about each of your personal finance positions and decide how you're going to split costs, contribute to savings, pay bills and set early goals in your relationship.

You mightn't follow these steps exactly, but this is what Sam and I did to lay our financial foundation. Success depends not just on the talk itself, but the setting, circumstances and approaches of when and how you have your chats.

Give a heads-up

If your partner walks in the door after a rough day, tired and stressed, this is probably not the time to start a cashflow conversation. Don't ambush your partner with a money talk. Isiah says this may make them feel like they've been 'been backed into a corner'.

Ideally, you'll agree on a day and time in advance, you might also establish a list of things each of you will have spent some time thinking about so that you're on equal footing and no one is caught off guard. In my case that meant making sure I had all of my major costs on hand to talk through.

When we wanted to get a clear picture of our shared financial position and future prospects, we talked about it at the start of the week and agreed to go out for dinner on Thursday night, so we had a few days to get ready. I told Sam I'd be bringing all of the information about the house and what it cost to manage it. I'd tell him how much money I had on hand for the renovation, and he'd be ready to tell me about his income, debt and regular expenses. Having an agreed time in the diary meant we both had time to prepare logistically and emotionally.

Know your objective

Perhaps you want to establish your household budget or set a shared goal. Regardless of the purpose of your conversation, aim to come away from the discussion with an outcome of some sort so that you don't go around in circles. With a clear objective, you'll then have a motivation to do the work required during your conversation to set yourself up for success.

For some topics, the discussion might take multiple conversations across several sessions. 'You might not get to your desired outcome on the first try; you don't have to have all of the answers at once,' Isiah says.

In our case, the objective for Sam and I was to gain a clear view of our financial situation and a rough plan for how we'd manage money in the next six months. There were still plenty of unknowns at that point, like how much it was going to cost to have some of the renovation work done, but we made good headway in that first discussion.

Manage the potential for conflict

You're both going to come at difficult conversations from a different perspective. It's likely you and your partner will operate on distinct frequencies. Isiah's tip is establishing beforehand that you can both ask for a 'time out' if you need to think about issues that arise. If things get heated and one person feels triggered or attacked, the outcome isn't going to be helpful, so know when to call a halt to the conversation and take some space.

Consider your location

If you're serious about improving your financial position together, give these conversations the time and energy they deserve. Remove any distractions like television and phones; being completely present shows your partner that you're serious and respectful of the conversation. You might even consider taking the chat outside of the house to a cafe or restaurant. That's not to say you need to spend a lot to have the discussion, but neutral turf can make a difference. We went to a local Chinese restaurant, but you can do it in a park, at the beach or any place where you can focus together.

Come with an open and optimistic mindset

A productive conversation requires the ability to truly listen and empathise with the other person's point of view. If you only intend to highlight your partner's downfalls, chances are you won't achieve what you hoped for. Make sure you can praise some great things about their approach to spending, saving or investing so they don't feel like they're under attack. Give your partner a chance to share their ideas. One of you might be 'better' at managing money, but thinking you've got all the answers will impact on the balance of power. You want equal ownership of the goal. As Isiah says, accepting your partner's influence and a willingness to compromise are essential.

Start with the good stuff

You don't need to launch into the numbers the moment you sit down. Take a moment to talk about the great aspects of your relationship, what you're excited about and why you think you're going to be better as a duo. Isiah believes a good way to begin is by 'starting with positive intentions, sharing an appreciation for your partner so they know you're working as a team and it's not one person versus the other'.

Knowing you're about to be vulnerable together can be really nerve-wracking regardless of your financial position. I was nervous to ask Sam about his income. It seemed like such an invasive thing to do, not least because I see him as so much more than any monetary contribution he makes to our lives. I was also concerned about sharing my own salary, how much the mortgage was, the impact of the interest rate that was steadily rising at the time, and how

I'd refinanced the property to get a small lump sum for the renovation. So, kicking off with some reinforcement of how much I valued him was just as important as the dollars and cents that would underpin the plan.

Let it all hang out

When we felt ready, I bit the bullet and talked him through my position first. I told him my salary, how much I made from extra freelance income and that I sometimes had a tax bill rather than a return due to the additional income. I shared what I'd paid for the house, how much the monthly repayments were, the current sum in the renovation fund and all of the expenses that came with the house: insurance, bills, council rates and so on. Then I told him about my other expenses including my car, health insurance, phone and internet. Given my outgoings, I wasn't saving much at all at that point.

I explained that although there was money in the reno fund, I didn't want to spend all of it. That it was important to have some buffer funds in case of emergency. But on the flipside, there were things that we needed to get done. When the property was in a suitable position, I wanted to have it revalued and consider the most effective way to manage repayments and interest rates from there. I told him that it could be stressful, that it often felt like a bigger burden than I could handle, but that I believed there was a huge amount of potential in the home.

When I was done, I was pleased to see he was still sitting there, tucking into a spring roll, holding my gaze and making it clear he'd understood everything I'd told him. Then it was his turn. He told me his income, what his expenses were and how much debt he had. He also told me why he had the debt, and it was no different to the reasons I'd taken on credit cards in the past – life sometimes throws curveballs, and he'd needed the funds to cover gaps when he'd moved or paid a bond. I got it because I'd been there too.

At that point, we worked out how much we made together and how much he'd contribute financially once his debt was clear. This was the point at which we agreed that I'd cover the mortgage completely for a few months so that we'd be debt-free moving forward (aside from our cars and the mortgage). He told me what he could do to minimise the impact on the renovation fund including replacing old floorboards, repairing damaged walls, painting and replacing old ceiling fans with new pendant lights.

We agreed on where we would spend money: professional sanding and polishing of the floorboards, and in six months, time, new carpet for a couple of bedrooms and some new curtains. As nice as a new kitchen would be, we'd wait until we could afford to do it properly. With that, we had a general plan in place. For now, we'd keep most of our finances separate. We'd already set up one joint account (a savings fund) and agreed to keep adding $25 per week each and reassess how we banked together down the track.

Set a goal

During that conversation, we set our first goal: to have most of the house painted, ceiling fans replaced with pendant lights and floors sanded and polished within six months. That would take us to the end of 2022, and we'd then establish what the next phase looked like. We went home pretty pumped and equally motivated. Sam was pleased to be kicking his debt and I was relieved that he wanted to play his part in the physical labour and the financial work needed to make the house a home we could both be proud of.

Your goal probably looks different to ours. Maybe you want to save a house deposit or start a business. Perhaps you want to work towards buying a car, take a holiday or open an investment account for your children. The goal itself doesn't matter, but hopefully you'll be equally excited by the prospect of achieving it.

Couples goals check-in

If you are keen to get better at discussing money, here are some questions to consider that could help you to build your confidence in having these chats, especially if you're in the early stages of dating. If you're not aligned on all your answers, it's not actually the end of the world. I'd be really surprised if both of you agreed on every answer. What's important is removing the taboo associated with bringing up money questions and working on the skill you need to negotiate different points of view.

Early questions for couples dating:

- What kind of experiences did you have with money growing up?
- What do you like spending spare cash on and why?
- What's your approach to spending, saving and investing?
- What does success look like to you?
- What's your dream lifestyle?
- What are your financial goals?

More in-depth questions for established couples:

- Will we plan to move in together? If so, will we rent or work towards buying our home?
- Will we always live in the same city or will we live elsewhere sometime?
- Are we happy in our respective industries or will we make changes in the future?

- What sort of holidays do we each like to take?
- How much is reasonable to spend on a holiday?
- How frequently do we intend to travel overseas?
- How much is reasonable to spend on cars?
- Will we invest together?
- Are there any significant ongoing personal expenses that one of us wants to keep up on our own?

CHAPTER THREE

Bling battles: why we fight over money

Hopefully by now you're feeling really well equipped to have an intimate chat about money with your partner. But as prepared as you are, that doesn't mean it's all sunshine and roses from here. Conflict and tension may arise as you talk about your financial future.

The results of a recent Australian survey indicate money is the root of many disputes in relationships. More than a third of those surveyed (35 per cent) said they had disagreements with their partner about money monthly, or more frequently, and four in five of those surveyed (80 per cent) agreed that financial issues were a leading cause of their relationship breakdown.

The results also showed that women were more likely to say that managing their financial situation had a negative impact on their health (45 per cent compared to 23 per cent). There's also a lot of secret-keeping when it comes to spending. Men were more likely than women to say that they kept secrets about money from their partner (42 per cent compared to 35 per cent) and those who identified as members of the LGBTIQA+ community were more likely than those who don't to say they are not comfortable having conversations with their partner about money (58 per cent compared to 36 per cent).

According to behavioural scientist and couples' therapist Lucille Shackleton, money is one of the six most common reasons that couples fight. Couple's therapist Isiah McKimmie says couples across the socioeconomic spectrum argue, and the amount of money you have isn't predictive of a great relationship. Even seriously rich people aren't exempt from squabbling about spending. That's because when you disagree about money, the conflict isn't actually about the money, it's what's happening underneath the issue.

Research from the Gottman Institute has found that money has up to 100 different meanings for people. Ultimately, fights about money aren't based on a dollar amount; they're usually about values.

I hate conflict, I don't know anyone who really loves it, but I generally try to avoid it. The problem with that is if someone is doing something that's bothering me, I won't address it with them. I'll let the issue fester and then lose it, usually at the most inappropriate time. This is something that

I'm working on, and I'm definitely getting better at it when it comes to my relationship with Sam. We're not immune to arguments; no one is. Fortunately, there are two reassuring things that happen during our disputes: we don't call each other names, and after having some time out, we always come back to one another quickly, take responsibility for our role in the issue and really talk out the problem at hand.

The values we all hold about money can often lead to disputes. For example, in the past I've had really bad emotional experiences as a result of being in credit card debt. It gave me anxiety and often made me feel powerless. I got in really deep and I continued to spend to keep up a lifestyle I'd created, which unsurprisingly made me feel worse and worse over time. I had to reach a breaking point to force a shift and once I was able to get out of the cycle, it was important to me to stay out. That meant completely altering my lifestyle, which in turn shifted my sense of self and my view of my future.

If Sam had said that he was comfortable with his debt or was considering going into more debt to make a big purchase, I'm guessing we would have argued about that. But the argument wouldn't have been about the debt itself; it would have happened because the idea of him not clearing a loan and potentially pursuing more debt would be bringing up a lot of emotions for me – emotions that had in the past resulted in a great deal of distress. Had this hypothetical debt been more important to him than my emotions, needs and values, we'd be headed towards conflict. But, on the flipside, I'd need to understand why this debt was important to him. Had it been to purchase tools for work, or complete further study because it was a really important goal, that'd be a whole other conversation.

In that scenario, you can see the surface issue is debt. But underneath it sits my anxiety and Sam's aspiration. A respectful, safe and considered discussion will reveal these things, so you can work out how to address the issue properly.

Money issues buried under a blanket

Sam and I became really good at talking about money in the first year of our relationship mostly because the subject of having to spend money came up *all* the time, as it tends to. Bills, car services, a problem with Sam's fuel tank, council rates, the absurd price of groceries, another interest rate rise, petrol, a new ladder, paint and two snags bought at Bunnings, how much we needed to spend on accommodation for upcoming weddings …

It's actually impossible not to talk about money with your partner. We talked plenty, but it took a massive fight over a blanket to get better communication and shared administration.

Here's what happened: we'd just had our floors sanded and polished. During the process we had all of our furniture stacked precariously in spare rooms. When the floors were done, we returned everything to its rightful place. I put my blanket back on the couch, but I didn't return Sam's. I didn't think we needed both, but it was a crappy move. His blanket was one of the few things in the room that belonged to him. Everything else had been chosen in my life before Sam.

An initially calm discussion escalated into something pretty dramatic.

But it wasn't about the blanket; a deep dive into the matter revealed that we both had to address the way in which we were still adjusting from our individualistic lifestyles and moving into a shared world.

As we batted our respective viewpoints back and forth, it became clear that there were many things we hadn't cemented in terms of each of us feeling like true equals.

We'd unconsciously slipped into equality in most aspects of our partnership when we were dating. Before moving in together, we split our time between my place and Sam's, we took it in turns to cook and clean, and we made an equal amount of effort to meet each other's family. But the day Sam moved into the house I'd bought, saying that I viewed it as ours now wasn't enough.

It was going to take time for that to truly be the case. Not only had Sam moved onto my turf, he was living in a renovation, so while he integrated some of his stuff with mine in the liveable rooms, a lot of his belongings went into the shed. Every single room in the house had my furniture in it, and spaces, such as the study, belonged entirely to me.

By contrast, Sam's clothes were in a spare room because we didn't have enough storage.

It wasn't fair, not least because he was slugging his guts out on the renovation.

But I didn't see this logically when we were in the depths of conflict. I became overwhelmed because on one hand I hated that I'd been so inconsiderate and selfish, wanting the room to look exactly as I desired. But I was also defensive. I had taken a terrifying leap of faith and bought a house with a hole in the bedroom floor and unplastered walls. To get something I could afford, I'd moved to an unfamiliar town, all with the hope that I might get ahead. I'd relentlessly questioned whether I'd made the right decision. I'd been lonely and, at times, depressed.

The stress of what I'd experienced prior to his arrival bubbled to the surface in the form of ugly tears. I had said I wanted it to be ours, but I had owned the angst and the weight of the responsibility before he arrived. I was carrying more of the mental load associated with interest-rate rises, bills and council rates.

We lost hours debating, walking away, coming back, talking again, more time apart followed by more talking before we eventually went to bed exhausted and calm, but not having reached a clear resolution.

It took until the next day for us to get to the root of the conflict. I told Sam that if he wanted more ownership of the house, I needed him to get more involved in the financial aspects of our life together. This meant not just contributing his share of money, but being engaged in the household admin in order to understand the impact of interest-rate rises and share the psychological burden of the total cost. He said that was reasonable, but in return he needed some ownership of the information that I managed, that he couldn't take on his share if he couldn't access it. It was pretty simple in the end, really.

Remarkably, a seemingly innocuous tussle over a blanket triggered an overhaul of the way we manage our finances. I put together a whole heap of files in a shared drive so that he could see our position clearly and access it any time he needed to. Shortly afterwards, we went to the bank and arranged joint access to an account that he was contributing to. We then made painting one of the unfinished rooms a priority so that he could move more of his stuff out of the shed. And Sam's blanket was returned to the couch.

The fight was beneficial in the respect that we made productive changes for both of us. But could we have handled it better? You're damn right we could have.

Managing conflicting goals

According to financial planner Rebecca Pritchard, sometimes when some couples sit down to talk specifically about their financial future, they leave the love and respect at the door: 'Because they're talking about money and suddenly it's a binary, blunt conversation.' But if you want to succeed in financial planning together, you've got to bring the love too.

She says that with couples, there are three people in the room, 'you', 'me', and 'us'. This means that the best way to work on your finances as a couple is to not just address the shared 'us' financial goals, but to give plenty of time and space to each individual's aspirations. Great couples still have their own objectives in life. At the end of the day, you still have an identity outside your relationship and it's both positive and healthy to want things for yourself.

Isiah McKimmie adds that to dissolve any conflict, you need to understand what's going on for your partner in terms of their money views and get a clear motivation for their need to save or spend on certain things. If you can do this, you'll be more likely to have a higher level of relationship satisfaction and be able to support each other's dreams, even if they're different.

But how different can those dreams be without the relationship imploding?

What if two people have completely conflicting aspirations? Like, one person wants to open their own cocktail bar, and the other wishes to travel to exotic locations around the world? It might sound like these lifestyle goals are mutually exclusive, but Isiah believes even seemingly opposing ambitions can be worked out. Communication and compromise are the keys. In this case, the couple might spend time locally while the bar is established and then take time out to travel when the place is humming along.

But what would happen if one person doesn't want to be a part of the other person's goal at all? What if one partner had no interest in travelling and the other doesn't want to pull late-night hospitality hours to support the cocktail bar? Isiah says a couple could still work through their differing agendas in order to make their respective goals achievable. Let's face it, you don't have to do *everything* together. In fact, all of the therapists I spoke with consistently reiterated the many benefits of pursuing goals independently, because it's actually good for your relationship. If you have a goal that you partner doesn't share, that's absolutely fine, as long as you're both open about the time, money and resources required. But, for it to work, the uninterested party can't stand in the way of your dream. They've got to back you.

It seems pretty obvious. I can't imagine being with someone who'd stand in the way of my personal goals, but it can happen when there are huge financial barriers to making it a reality. Regardless of what your personal or shared goals are, Isiah advises that the more you discuss the hurdles, the more likely you are to find workable solutions.

But why? Interrogating your goals

A key part of getting on the same page as you plan your financial future is building enough self-awareness to know not only what you aim to do with your hard-earned coin, but *why* you want to do it. Motivation isn't intrinsic from birth; it's born out of experience. According to behavioural scientist and couples' therapist Lucille Shackleton, the way money is used can become an internalised belief. A person from a family of spenders may associate spending money with love. But another person may be more concerned with security and therefore wish to save money. When you have two different approaches to money, one individualistic and another communal, the communal partner may feel unloved because their partner doesn't want to spend money.

Lucille points out that 'this will feel quite threatening' and destabilising to the partner who sees spending money as a way of showing love and therefore feels they're not having their needs met. It might sound superficial, but it's really a reflection of the value that was given to money and the way that it becomes internalised. These issues are likely to keep reappearing unless both people in a partnership are able to do the work required to understand their money psychology.

Returning to the communication skills discussed in chapter two, reflecting on and sharing your childhood money experiences often helps unearth the values driving your goals. You can create empathy by working to understand each other's money psychology and how it drives decision-making. Depending on the family finances of your youth, you may have internalised fear or confidence surrounding money. Talking through the topics from chapter two will help you to understand the 'why' that motivates you in both your individual and shared aspirations. A compelling 'why' helps to frame the importance of the goal. In turn, this hopefully helps you to navigate disagreements about how to spend, save or invest with perhaps more ease and sensitivity than you have in the past.

Tips for managing conflict

If you're in a long-term relationship, you're going to disagree occasionally. Sometimes it'll be a niggle over what to have for dinner, and at other times it might be over the unnecessarily colourful language your partner uses while watching the footy. Or it could be a passionate debate about a life-altering choice for you as a couple. The seriousness of your conflicting views will vary, but there are healthy strategies that you can use to minimise the potential for damage and disconnection in your relationship.

Simply knowing these tools are available to you and getting better at identifying when to use them can make a huge difference to the way that you work through and resolve conflicting views before the issue escalates into a full-blown drama.

Use I statements rather than You statements

If you're not agreeing on your couple goals, there are things you can do to prevent each other from going into fight or flight mode and steer the conversation back to productive territory. Isiah says it's powerful to 'speak from the perspective of *I* rather than *you*'.

Example I statements:

- I'm concerned about how much we spend on the weekend.
- I would like to make sure we're planning ahead really well.

Example You statements:

- You spend a lot more than I do.
- You forget to pay bills on time.

'You' statements make your partner feel defensive, whereas putting yourself in the statement by using 'I' helps you to express how you feel without casting blame. But statements about how you're feeling aren't always enough; asking questions that enable your partner to feel heard are also helpful.

Questions that can help you to get to a shared position

- Can you help me to understand your perspective?
- Can you tell me why that's important to you?
- What feelings do you have about this?
- Does this relate to your past experiences?

Use active listening

Lucille says a big part of having a productive argument is being able to actively listen to the other person. That means going beyond hearing the words, to really making an effort to understand the meaning your partner is trying to convey. In other words, putting your phone down and facing your partner, making eye contact, asking questions and refraining from passing judgement while they explain their position.

Sounds easy enough, but it can be tough in the heat of the moment, especially if you reckon you have good reason to be pissed off. Still, pay closer attention to how well you're listening next time an exchange becomes heated. Biting your tongue could make all the difference.

Validate their emotions

Once you've heard their view, Lucille says it's important to 'validate their perspective and their emotions', which doesn't mean you need to agree with their point. Validating is not the same as agreeing. 'A lot of people can sit in the discomfort of not agreeing but as long as they're seen, heard and understood, they're okay,' she says.

Look under the surface

If you're at a stalemate over a money-related issue, shift the goal posts and work to understand why you each hold a particular opinion. As we've discussed, it's never just about the money; it's about the dreams, beliefs and values behind it.

This is often the case when one person really won't budge. If someone won't compromise, it may be that they have a strong internalised belief from childhood that they're unaware of and can't shake. If you can identify what's going on below the surface, you may be able to find a resolution sooner.

Recognise escalation

We all know it's rare for good things to come out of a nasty, ugly fight. If you feel the discussion escalating, you'll hopefully spot it before it blows up, at which point you might take a break. You can always set a timeframe to come back to it when temperatures and voices have returned to a simmer. This is an important distinction to walking away or withdrawing for an extended period. Lucille suggests saying to your partner: 'I'm really overwhelmed right now, and this is not a productive conversation. Let's take an hour and come back to it. I'm going to go for a walk.'

Find the sweet spot

But how do you move forward once you've returned from your break? Ideally you've had time to think about the problem objectively. Lucille's recommendation when it comes to resolving conflict associated with a big financial decision is talking honestly about what's best for the relationship and what's best financially. In turn, you can hopefully find a middle ground that's ideally not going to do serious harm to your relationship, or your bank account.

Fight fair

It's all well and good to say there's an optimal way to deal with conflict, but sometimes things get dirty. You might raise an issue from ages ago or have a personal dig that's unrelated to the issue at hand. We all say things we regret during lover's quarrels. But there are some things you can actively avoid that could do serious damage to your relationship. It can be much harder to repair if you use personal criticism to point-score your way out of an argument.

Contempt is similarly dangerous. You really want to avoid mocking, sarcasm and condescending actions including rolling your eyes and sneering because that will induce lingering tension. Side note: contempt doesn't just show up in conflict; it's any form of disrespect that implies you're superior. If you chip away at your partner's self-worth by devaluing their presence in your life, you're seriously risking your couple goals and your relationship's future.

Finally, getting defensive, completely shutting down or stonewalling doesn't end an argument; it prolongs it. Walking away may be an attempt to stop any further escalation in a disagreement, but shutting down likely makes your partner feel isolated and potentially angrier. There's a huge difference between taking a break to calm down and using silent treatment indefinitely. If you need time out, say so but make sure it has an end point. You then need to come back to the conversation, open and willing to give the discussion another shot, otherwise you're in danger of making a deeper wound.

Couple goals check-in

You mightn't want to pick at old battle scars by discussing previous fights, particularly those you've since resolved, but there are some things you can ask yourself that help you to reflect on your own patterns of behaviour so that you're better placed to disagree productively next time.

- In your last disagreement about money, did you get to the root of the issue by establishing if there was a value sitting beneath the surface?
- To what extent do you use 'I' statements rather than 'you' statements?
- Do you fight fair? Or do you use tactics that do more harm than good?
- Do you understand each other's money psychology?
- What kinds of beliefs and values do you both hold?

CHAPTER FOUR

Financial housekeeping: cleaning up your banking

I'll chat with Sam about lifestyle goals and dreams any chance I get, but working out how we'd manage banking and the associated life admin did my head in. Before Sam and I moved in together, I asked so many couples: how do you handle your banking? Who pays for what? Everyone had a different answer, and in most cases, it had taken a stack of trial and error before they found their rhythm. The responses also varied depending on the phase they were in. The topic of bank accounts can be polarising. Some people swear by going all-in, others had entirely separate accounting systems. Many took a hybrid approach as they navigated their financial journey together, meaning some costs were shared and others were kept separate. When it came to shared costs, some split everything 50/50, others paid a percentage of the cost depending on who earned more. So, for example, they might split costs 60/40 if one person earned more. Others set up agreements where one person paid the rent or mortgage, and the other paid the utilities. In another case, one paid all of the household expenses, and the other paid for the childcare.

Very early in our relationship, Sam and I set up a shared account and agreed to contribute $25 each per week. The idea was that it would be an amount that could have easily been wasted on a couple of coffees here and there, but over time we'd see it grow. It was also the beginning of an important habit: saving together. To begin with we didn't really have a plan for the fund – loosely it was for a holiday or a special occasion.

At the time, Sam was paid at the beginning of each week while I was paid monthly and also had occasional freelance income, so when I got the notification that he'd contributed his share, usually while I was at my desk, and he was about to head home from the site he was landscaping, I'd add my portion and he'd get a notification too. We didn't have to say a word, the action said: Mondays suck, but we're $50 bucks closer to cocktails by a pool sometime in the future.

We then had the big transparent conversation, openly outlining our income and expenses, so that we could set our first goals, as discussed in chapter two. Although we had agreed on shared goals, in those early months our financial administration was entirely separate, and we'd transfer cash back and forth to each other as needed.

After we had our fight about the blanket, we became a lot better at the shared administration, but the evolution of our financial arrangement didn't stop there.

We'd agreed that it was best that Sam took the lead on the renovation project management – everything from sourcing reclaimed Baltic pine floorboards that suited the style of our home to deciding how we'd tackle the work needed in each room of the house. That's not to say I sat back and did nothing, but it's his strength – he's the tradie. I had absolutely no business telling him how to take out old ceiling fans or cut floorboards to the right length. I do, however, listen when he's teaching me a new skill. I mightn't be the lead on the physical labour, but I've learned how to use an orbital sander and my painting skills have improved drastically under Sam's watch.

On the flipside, I'm responsible for paying our bills on time and I manage the budget to make sure we're on track. But we discuss big purchases at length before things are paid for. We've decided this is how we work best. Someone has to take a backseat, or take direction, while the other leads in various aspects of our lives together. We know where our strengths lie. In my case that means being fairly certain that I'll never go up into the roof to see how the lights are connected. In Sam's case it means trusting me to stay on top of our financial housekeeping.

But expecting one person in the relationship to be 100 per cent accountable for a huge aspect of the relationship could lead to resentment later. I don't expect Sam to do all of our renovation on his own just because he's more skilled. I have a responsibility to learn as we go and do my share. Similarly, I don't want to do the money stuff on my own all the time – I need him to be across what's happening too. We know that if we want to achieve our couple goals, we've both got to do our share of the work, even in the areas that aren't our strengths.

Still, this has been challenging at times. We had to learn – the hard way – that being the lead on our respective areas didn't mean the other person could turn a blind eye to the stuff they weren't responsible for.

Initially, when quotes for renovation work came in, I'd say, 'Yep, that's great. Tell them we're happy to go ahead.' And Sam would do it. But Sam didn't have any real visibility of the numbers. I'd just mention in passing how much we had available to do jobs. After the disagreement we'd recently had over the blanket, it was clear this wasn't cutting it. He needed access to the renovation fund because he was booking in trades and buying hardware supplies.

But there's a reason I didn't go out of my way to give him access from the get-go.

Prior to meeting Sam, I had refinanced the property and accessed equity in the home to get the renovation funds, so this wasn't just a few hundred bucks; it was thousands. Setting up access meant going to the bank and giving Sam 'authority to act' on the account, meaning he could freely buy things and pay tradespeople's invoices without my permission.

He couldn't be expected to contribute to the costs of the renovation and run the project management without access to the transactions and balance. But this is not something I would have done if I didn't trust him entirely.

We were very clear that this account was strictly for costs associated with the house, but there was nothing stopping either of us from withdrawing all of it and taking off to another country, gambling it away or going on a shopping spree.

Neither of us were doing that, of course, but it's a risk that any joint bank account holders run. In the wrong hands, ownership of the household finances can be dangerous.

Spotting financial abuse red flags

According to a 2022 report, more than 623,100 people were subjected to financial abuse in Australia in 2020 – one in 30 women, and one in 50 men.

Forms of financial abuse included being a victim of a partner who did not contribute to household expenses, having income withheld or controlled by an abusive partner, having a partner who didn't meet the financial needs of dependants, or being prevented from working.

The cumulative cost of withholding or controlling a victim's incomes or finances was $3.2 billion. This doesn't include other forms of abuse or the broader economic, social and mental-health costs.

I'm telling you this because whether you love a budgeting spreadsheet or you'd rather let your partner oversee the household accounting, allowing one person to have too much authority, or making assumptions about how money is being spent, can lead to financial abuse in the worst-case scenario.

But, by contrast, there's financial independence to consider. I'm big on individuals maintaining some level of financial independence, even if they've been in a relationship for decades. Income transparency is usually a positive in a relationship, however, financial advisor Jessica Brady tells me it can be 'unsafe for women to be overt about how much they earn, as women who earn more have a higher chance of experiencing domestic violence'. According to the Australian Bureau of Statistics, a woman who earns more than a male partner is 35 per cent more likely to experience domestic violence.

Forensic accountant Suzanne Delbridge is called on by the courts to track down money and assets during separations and divorces. She sees people hiding money regularly. 'In all but the most amicable cases, people have an agenda to get the most out of the settlement that they can.'

In divorce proceedings, she's observed that when there is one person who is largely in control of finances, they will 'try to minimise what's there' so that the other person potentially misses out on cash and assets in the settlement. Far from being something out of a movie, people really do send money to Swiss bank accounts and redistribute assets to relatives living overseas.

Unfortunately, this is still a blatantly gendered issue with more men hiding assets than women. In such situations this is a delicate path to walk because financial abuse is often tied to verbal or physical abuse.

So, is there any way for people to prevent themselves from getting to this point? Yes, and it's essential to pick up on the signs early.

Control over banking

If you don't have access to banking and financial statements that impact you, that's your first sign that something's up. At a minimum, you need to know where to log into accounts and you should freely be able to see transactions at any time. This is particularly important if you're a spouse who's not working for one reason or another. Suzanne uses the example of people who've stopped working to care for children and their partner gives them an allowance rather than access to all bank accounts. If you don't have a full understanding of your financial position, 'that would be a red flag,' she says.

Small business ambiguity

It's one thing to be in a situation where you and your partner have fairly straightforward salaried roles, but things become more complex when you have a small business. A sign that there might be a problem is when you ask how the business is going and the response is something along the lines of 'You don't need to know'. But, that said, if you're not across the detail of how the business works, or how it's being run, Suzanne says it's hard to work out what information to ask for and this can be exacerbated when you are asked to sign documents.

Transparency is key. You must be engaged with financial matters that impact you. That's as simple as being involved if your partner prepares tax returns on your behalf. Even if it's not your strength, it's essential to pay attention when you go to the accountant and 'keep copies of your own documents'. Remaining engaged when finance doesn't come naturally to you can be a challenge, but you must maintain a level of transparency that both protects you and helps you to grow as a couple. There's a big difference between being a 'financial team captain' and knowing what's happening. According to financial planner Rebecca Pritchard, it's really common for one person to do most of the financial administration. She suggests that as long as the other person still has a voice and contributes to the decision-making, 'that's okay, and very normal'.

Know where to find your money

Rebecca also observes that one of the keys to avoiding financial abuse isn't necessarily having a separate stash of cash hidden away, it's knowing where the money is in the first place. Saying 'I'm not a money person, my partner manages our cash' is potentially more concerning than not having an emergency fund of your own.

She argues that the best thing you can do to protect yourself from financial vulnerability is to ensure that you don't relinquish financial control. If you know where all of your income is, what bills you have and understand how the cashflow works, 'all of those steps are natural insurance policies against financial abuse in themselves'.

If financial abuse is a concern, maintain a separate account

Depending on the circumstances, some people will need or want an entirely separate account, particularly if they have a history of abuse or poor relationships. In these cases, you might consider setting up individual buffer funds so that each person has their own emergency money that is entirely in their control. It depends on each person's personal history, financial literacy and specific needs.

Should you pool all your money?

A 2022 study out of Cornell University indicated that couples who pool their money are less likely to break up. The study projected that pooled finances would lead to an increase in dependence on each other but instead the research showed that couples who held everything jointly tended to have a better connection and more positive, stable and safe interactions.

And yet, this doesn't account for people who do go all-in only to end up struggling to leave a relationship if they need to because their spending can be tracked. Then there's potential disputes that arise out of how money should be spent on personal priorities. I don't want to have to explain every single purchase I make to Sam, nor do I expect that of him. I also wonder how people buy Christmas and birthday presents and maintain some mystery when their partner can easily view every aspect of their transaction history.

So, what's the best way for a couple to manage their banking? Is it best to have everything in a joint bank account to streamline your administration? Do you keep most finances separate to maintain your sense of self? Or is there a healthy middle ground?

Enmeshment vs interdependence

Behavioural scientist and couples' therapist Lucille Shackleton believes that it can be useful not just to look at the administration associated with money in a relationship, but also the dynamic of your partnership. Often in relationships, couples will fall into enmeshment or interdependence.

In a relationship, enmeshment involves ambiguous boundaries in which one or both people lose much of their autonomy, make all choices together and consistently need one another's validation. In turn each person's identity and ambitions may be significantly diminished. We all know couples who regularly and proudly announce they can't live without each other. That's not necessarily a good thing.

When enmeshment occurs, their individual identities can fade. You may frequently put your partner's needs ahead of your own and disregard your personal needs. In the extreme, couples may take on each other's emotions and can lose their own sense of self, which can in turn have mental and emotional impacts and lead to social anxiety, depression and co-dependency.

In fact, Lucille claims enmeshment can lead to a loss of intimacy and passion, which is why she advocates for interdependence. This means being confident that you can depend on one another, but you also have a clear sense of self and plenty of autonomy. This can also apply to finances, because if everything is intertwined, and you don't have an ability to pay for things from your own personal account, you may begin to rely on the other person entirely.

Instead, you want to strive for interdependence. Meaning, you of course value your emotional and intimate connection, but you still have a clear sense of self. That's why experts recommend striking a balance between having some money shared while still allowing for at least a portion of financial independence.

So it's fine to have joint bank accounts and things you're working on together but you still want to maintain some sense of independence. You don't want to lose yourself in the relationship.

Lucille says financial transparency 'diffuses the potential for power and control later and creates equality which is really good for a relationship'. The way you store your income may be less important than the decisions you make regarding how to use it, particularly when it comes to your long-term vision. 'Money is connected with hopes and dreams, so making decisions together is beneficial,' she says.

But what about the way people choose to spend the money that they keep separate? Is buying whatever you want with your individual funds fair game? Lucille believes it's important to be transparent about things that affect the other person. This includes significant purchases and personal debt. Ultimately she suggests that you don't have to share details about absolutely every purchase, but if it's going to affect the other person then it's respectful to discuss it first.

CASE STUDY

Twenty-nine-year-old Victorian Olivia is a teacher and social media content creator. Olivia says that when she met her partner, who lived in the same area as her, she was quite well established financially before they got together. Olivia had purchased her home solo about a year prior to their meeting. Having worked hard to obtain it, she naturally felt a need to look after the home, which is still in her name only, without compromising the relationship. She found the process interesting as the party who owned a property. It was difficult to achieve a fair arrangement while also protecting assets and emotions.

Olivia's partner had no assets other than some savings when they moved in together. They shacked up pretty quickly out of necessity during the pandemic, so they kept their finances mostly separate. They agreed that he would give her $800 a month to cover rent and bills. This strategy, which lasted about a year, worked for them. In 2022, they started contributing $200 each per fortnight to a joint account for groceries and the occasional takeaway meal. According to Olivia, combining some money and keeping most separate is a model that works well for them.

It's something they review regularly though. When interest rates rose steadily in mid-late 2022, her partner began increasing his rental contribution to account for the mortgage repayment hike so they could 'both take on the burden of the increases'.

Because they've successfully and respectfully navigated their money management, the experience has had a positive impact on Olivia's partner. He has quite a lot of money in shares now and that is solely his. He has also started out-earning her, so things have balanced out.

They are both fairly free and generous with their money, but they both have their own investing goals so they do this separately.

As their relationship develops, Olivia anticipates that they will merge their finances more over time, because they have similar goals and spending habits, so she feels comfortable with a future integration.

That said, they have also discussed what would happen if they ever split up. The house would be Olivia's as she pays the mortgage, insurance, rates and maintenance. Their individual shares are separate, and they would leave with what they have. This includes their super and cars.

Joint bank account considerations

Of all of the professionals I've spoken with, no one insisted that there is a right way to manage bank accounts, but most advocated for a form of hybrid that works for you as a couple. The hybrid has several benefits. First, it gives both of you transparency and accountability for shared expenses, but it also allows for each individual to maintain their autonomy and avoid complete enmeshment. Importantly, in the event that one person wants to leave a relationship that becomes unhealthy, dangerous or financially abusive, it allows them to do so.

On the other hand, opening a joint bank account is not something you need to rush into. Trust is imperative. If your partner is pressuring you to open a joint account and close your personal accounts entirely, that's a red flag. A joint account comes with a shared responsibility for the debt and expenses accrued. If your partner takes on debt that they can't pay off, it's on both of you. Similarly, if they take the money and spend it, you can't get it back.

Here are the main types of joint accounts that you might consider:

Both to sign

Some financial institutions allow you to set up an account that requires both of you to grant permission before a purchase is made. This can be advantageous from a safety perspective, but not necessarily convenient if you want to nip out to buy milk and bread.

Either to sign

Most accounts are set up as a default 'either to sign' which means either of you can pay bills and make purchases without the other person's permission.

Third-party authority

This is where one of you already has an account open and you give your partner authority to use it – it's much like an 'either to sign' account, except in most cases the original account holder can remove access that was granted to the third-party at any time if they need to.

The expert approach

Financial planner Rebecca Pritchard and her husband's salaries get paid into the same joint account. With the total income, they then disperse funds to several accounts, including their savings, investments and regular repayments. They also put cash into an account for their child-related expenses. Finally, Rebecca has an account in her name and so does her husband, and each month they contribute a slice of total earnings to their own needs.

In Rebecca's example, she highlights the fact that while she does have her own account, the money that goes into it comes from their joint account. There is a difference between perceived autonomy and actual autonomy. Rebecca says, 'Most people, when they break it down, are happy with perceived autonomy. I have perceived autonomy in that I have my money and I can do whatever I want with it. At the end of the day it's coming from a joint place, but it's as fair as we're happy for it to be at this point. This is the path that most of my clients take. Very few people say "no this is mine and that's yours, stay over there".'

Hybrid harmony

Six months into our relationship, Sam and I had settled on a hybrid approach. This would evolve further over time, and we'll explore that in a future chapter, but here's how it looked at that point.

Pocket-money fund: the savings habit-builder

This is the account that we put $25 into each week. Initially, the plan was to build it up and then spend it on a holiday or a little luxury, but interestingly, while I was the one who set it up with a view to treating ourselves, Sam would go on to insist we didn't touch it if we didn't have to. That small sum turned into thousands in the first year. We liked the way this simple habit had a big impact – seeing the buffer grow over time was really rewarding.

The practical fund: weekly food and drinks

In this account we added $150 each per week to cover food, drinks and a bit of shared entertainment. Initially, we just took it in turns to pay for things and generally we thought costs were split fairly, but we never stopped to count dollar for dollar. I was pretty loose with my spending on food, but with this system in place, if we got to the end of the weekend and had, say, $30 left in the account, we challenged ourselves not to go over and make any remaining meals with this sum. By contrast, if we had more, that stayed in the account and we added another $150 on Monday regardless, so we'd have extra cash for the next week. This fund kept us both accountable.

The home fund: mortgage and renovations

This is the account that I had before I met Sam, which he started contributing to and has access to. It's the mortgage offset account, meaning money in this fund offsets interest paid on the mortgage, so the more in it, the better. That's why we agreed Sam would pay his share of household costs into this fund, rather than transferring to my personal account. During this time, we paid household bills and managed the renovation costs with this account. In our first year together, this was the big fund that we put as much into as we could, as it's how we bankrolled our long-term goals.

The individual funds: our own money

These are the accounts that we use for personal spending, which allows us to maintain our autonomy. It means if either of us go out with friends, we don't have to justify how much was spent. We like being able to buy our own stuff with our hard-earned coin. The caveat being that spending from our personal accounts never comes at the expense of our long-term goals.

You do you

All that said, I can understand why some people still go all-in with one joint bank account, particularly once they have a family or if there's only one income. But this is the choice we made to maintain a balance between working together and having autonomy in the first year of our relationship. As with all aspects of our shared finances, we expected the way we managed money to be further refined with time. What's important is that we had set up a structure that worked for us in the early stages of our relationship and we continued to talk regularly about what we needed to do to keep it working effectively.

Couples and tax

It does get increasingly difficult to maintain autonomy when you live together, as being a couple impacts your tax status. Accountant Julian Mauro says you aren't bound together with tax implications from the day you make it official but, importantly, you don't have to be married to be up for shared tax obligations.

What you need to consider is the definition of a spouse. In your tax return, you'll need to state how many days you had your 'spouse' in a given financial year. According to Julian, 'This is self-assessed, so you need to put what you think is correct.' Generally speaking, Julian suggests that 'once you move in together and have shared bank accounts, [that] is likely to be the start date'.

Why does it matter? Well, your tax return is assessed on whether you're a single person or a couple. Your relationship status will impact considerations such as the Medicare levy surcharge that is payable if you don't have private health insurance. At the time of writing, singles earning more than $93,000 and couples earning more than $186,000 will pay the Medicare levy surcharge, and the family income cap increases by $1500 for each dependent after the first child.

There are some nuances, though. For example, if you had a spouse for a full financial year and your family income exceeded the threshold but your own income was $23,365 or less, you don't have to pay the surcharge. Additionally, if you and your partner become spouses during the course of the year, or you separate, you might pay the surcharge for the days you were single if your own income was more than $93,000. Similarly, you might be liable for the portion of the year that you were in a spousal relationship and your family income exceeded $186,000. Ultimately, the amount you need to pay will be based on the information that both of you provide in your tax returns.

Here are the ATO thresholds and associated surcharges at a glance.

Threshold	Base tier	Tier 1	Tier 2	Tier 3
Single threshold	$93,000 or less	$93,001 – $108,000	$108,001 – $144,000	$144,001 or more
Family threshold	$186,000 or less	$186,001 – $216,000	$216,001 – $288,000	$288,001 or more
Medicare levy surcharge	0 per cent	1 per cent	1.25 per cent	1.5 per cent

'Ideally, for full tax maximisation you'd both want to have the same level of hospital cover once you're disclosing a spouse in your tax return,' Julian says. In short: if you move in with your partner and you work out that between the two of you you'll earn more than $186,000, you'll likely be better off at tax time if you have private health insurance.

Couple goals check-in

We've heard a lot about the many different ways to manage money and design your bank accounts as a couple in this chapter. Perhaps it's frustrating that we're not wrapping up this section with a clear set of instructions for how to put a money-management structure in place, but what you now have is a series of considerations for how you view your banking, both individually and together, along with thought-starters for how your incomes may contribute to your overall wealth-building capacity.

- Are we both happy with the way that our bank-account management is structured?
- Are we financially enmeshed or interdependent?
- Are our bank accounts set up in a way that allows us to achieve our personal and shared goals?
- Do we understand our tax obligations as a couple?
- How do we manage our regular bills (are they automated or is one of us responsible)?
- How do we split costs – 50/50 or as a percentage of each of our respective incomes?
- Do we have a joint account and our own individual accounts or is everything in one location?
- How much should we generally spend on food and entertainment each week?
- How much should each of us contribute to our shared savings?

CHAPTER FIVE

Values, goals and shared visions

I have to be honest: I've never really loved the concept of structured 'goal setting'. I think goal setting, like budgeting, can be pretty rigid and there's no one-size-fits all approach that is realistically going to suit everyone. In the past, I've thrived best when I've given myself a ridiculous financial goal to achieve in a short timeframe and then sacrificed myself silly or side-hustled until I've collapsed to get there.

The times I have pulled off wild, seemingly impossible financial goals have always been the occasions when there was a really strong 'why' motivating me. The most obvious was my house deposit. My 'why' was a home. Underneath that was some of my key values: safety, stability and security. My commitment to not living in a dodgy sharehouse ever again was also a pretty strong motivator.

Financial goals can be a lot like New Year's resolutions. If you don't have a 'why' and a value sitting under your goal, the incentive to achieve it is unclear. For example, let's say I want to save $6,000 this year. I could aim to put away $500 each month, or $16 every single day, but if I don't have any plans for that $6,000, I can almost guarantee that I'm going to fall short, and justify spending money on other things or simply lose interest in the goal.

Similarly, if your goal is to 'get rich', the question that follows has to be 'why'? Is it because you value freedom to live your life without the need for traditional employment? Or because you want enough money to ensure that your children are always well taken care of? A bit of introspection might help you to firm up *why* you want to get rich.

The upside of interrogating your *why* is you might not actually need as much as you think you do. You mightn't need millions to live a happy life aligned with your values. The cash you make is the conduit to the life you want, and you can't work out how much you need if you don't know what you value.

Values

According to financial advisor Jess Brady, the most successful financial-planning process begins by understanding each individual's values. 'Couples often don't know what is important to them on an individual level. Your core values drive your behaviour and often couples don't know if they have competing or conflicting values.'

Identifying your values can help each of you to become more conscious of your money philosophy. This exercise can be illuminating.

Your values will have a direct impact on the way you save, spend and invest. For example, if one of you values freedom above all else, you will spend or invest according to that value. If you see value in safety and security, you may be more focused on developing a strong savings buffer and want a home that provides a roof over your head and the stability that comes with it.

If your values aren't aligned, you're likely to be met with challenges. Jess says that in the case of coupled-up clients she's had who've since split, 'there was a huge unresolved value conflict'.

Chances are you don't often stop to think about your values and how you want to apply them to your financial life.

If you're not sure what your values are, here are some examples to get you started:

Time: perhaps you want more time to spend with family and friends, or you desire more hours for creativity and leisure.

Security: you might have experienced periods of instability, so you crave the safety and stability of savings and housing.

Generosity: many people grew up in environments where money was something that was shared to support family, so you like to have enough to give freely.

Independence: in this case you need the space and freedom to live life on your terms and may be working towards financial freedom that helps you to achieve this.

Family: you like to make your parents, siblings, children and partner a priority and seek to set up a lifestyle that supports this.

Personal growth: this might come in the form of education, career and exploration of hobbies and passions.

You may have other values or identify with one or more of these. Once you know what you value you can begin to assess whether the way you use money reflects these values. Jess says that if you haven't given much space to your value system, you may be behaving unconsciously and in turn this might be having an impact on your relationship. As you spend more time thinking about and discussing your values, you'll get better at setting shared goals together.

With a clear set of individual and shared values in place, couples can then 'put a structure in place' to ensure they're working to meet their value needs and those of their partner. From here, you're well placed to set financial goals that allow you to decide what to prioritise for yourself, and as a pair, ensuring you've been mindful of your values and your 'why'.

Like all aspects of life, financial goals aren't static, though. According to Jess, 'they live, breathe and iterate'.

Your values and priorities will inevitably evolve with age and experience, you're not locking yourself into a value system for eternity, but periodically stopping to see if your goals are aligned with your values may help you to course correct as needed.

Living in alignment with your values

After establishing your values, you'll be able to see if you're both living in alignment with the things you deem important today and also see if you're on track to achieve your short and long-term goals.

Here's an example:

Let's say your value is time. Today, that might be enough time to spend with your partner and also work on an art project. Long-term, you might aspire to have the time to become an artist and pursue that vocation without the constraints of a full-time job.

In that case, your financial goal is probably going to be building assets, getting rid of any debt you might have and building a passive income through shares, property or a combination of both. If so, Jess suggests that you need to work out how many assets and how much passive income you need to make that goal a reality and you then 'tie a monetary target to the goal'.

For example, you might work out that you need a million dollars worth of property and shares. From your position today, Jess says you can then see the gap between your current position and how long it could take you to hit your target.

Perhaps you want to travel around Australia in a van and your partner wants to spend a year living in New York. You can use financial modelling to see what can and can't be done. In the case where two people have conflicting goals, Jess suggests asking yourselves, 'Of these things, which would make you really sad if they never happened?'

Through that lens, you decide together. Perhaps you can live without a year in New York. Instead you might be content to have a month-long holiday there sometime. But you do want to get to the point where you can live as an artist and travel around Australia, so you trade off the bigger house and the better car and live a bit more frugally now to achieve these things.

It's a financial advisor's job to help people identify the risks and pitfalls of their goals and to develop different investment strategies to help them succeed. The more specific you are with your financial targets, the better your chance of success. According to Jess, 'If you have wishy-washy goals, it's harder to plan.'

While individual and shared goals vary from couple to couple, she says that you both need to be emotionally invested and truly motivated if you want a serious shot at achieving them. 'If one person abdicates, it's an unfair burden for the other person to shoulder.'

The way that you plan to achieve your goals in the present will depend on what works best for you as a couple, but a good way to start is by working out how much it costs you to live, how much you need for discretionary spending and then 'pooling everything else and deploying it to goals'.

Finally, couples should revisit their goals at regular intervals – monthly or quarterly, for example. This is an opportunity to review your current position, see how you're tracking and find ways to improve.

Applying your values to your goals

When we think about the goals and dreams we're working towards as individuals and couples, Lucille says that the Gottman Institute's 'sound relationship house' is an ideal reference to consider. You can google the house to see the key levels. At the bottom of the house, you need foundations such as trust and commitment; you can't put the roof on until you have these. But for our purposes, we're going to focus on the top two levels: making life dreams come true and creating shared meaning.

On the 'making dreams come true' level, you focus on the objectives you set together, from paying off debt to supporting one another to achieve professional aspirations.

While on the top level, the ultimate aspiration is creating shared meaning. The meaning is found in the things that give your relationship its identity. It's the 'rituals of connection' that form the inner world of your relationship.

Meaning can be found in the smallest things – taking it in turns to make the morning coffees – and as big as working on a significant goal together.

In the case of setting financial goals and working towards them, you're simultaneously on a path to making your life dreams come true and creating the shared meaning that helps you to maintain your bond.

But where do you start if you have a sense of your values and don't know what your financial goals are?

Goal setting

Start by talking about your goals. It's not something that you need to do as soon as you start dating, but behavioural scientist and couples' therapist Lucille Shackleton suggests, 'As things become serious, you might want to think about creating some shared goals, while also talking about how you can support each other to achieve individual goals.'

The goal doesn't have to be financially overt in nature. You don't necessarily need to be working towards making a million dollars, for example. Instead, ask, 'What's behind the goal?' Getting to the desire that's fuelling it will tell you a lot about where to place the goal in terms of your financial priorities.

So, this means coming back to a value. It might be creating security for yourselves, or a safe space for children to grow up. In this case the value is safety and security and therefore the financial goal might be to buy a house that provides that.

Value = safety and security

Goal = buy a house

With a value that underpins a goal in place, you're then able to break down your goal into achievable milestones. These might include researching dwelling types and prices in your preferred area, saving a deposit in a given timeframe, engaging a mortgage broker and getting yourself into a position where you can start making offers.

If you have different money values, where one person wants safety and security and the other values freedom and adventure, for example, you may find that the second person is less interested in prioritising saving for a house deposit because they want to travel. So, although you mightn't want to bring up a strong desire for safety and security on a first date, keeping an eye on your partner's values is something to do reasonably early, because a significant value conflict can create issues if you get to the point where you're planning the future and you have entirely different lifestyle objectives.

Lucille cautions: value-based disparity is something you need to be aware of, even in those heady early days of your love story. 'If your values are too vastly different, you need to ask yourself, "Is this going to make my life really hard?"'

If you want to buy a house for safety and security and your partner can't or won't get on board, that's not only going to make your goal much harder to achieve, it's a threat to your values. A cavernous gap between your individual values and goals is unlikely to lead to a happy financial or personal relationship.

Conflicting values and goals

In the case of significantly different values and goals, successful couples will come up with a compromise. Where one person values safety and security and the other values freedom and adventure, one might ask, 'Can we travel for a couple of years then come back and settle down?' That can work, because it's possible to value safety, security, freedom and adventure, it's just that you value safety and security above freedom and adventure, or vice versa.

This is the nature of being in a relationship. You can't go doing all of the things you want, whenever you want, as a single individual can. There's no one-size-fits-all approach when it comes to compromise. Lucille says, 'It's about finding that middle ground between the goals or dreams and coming up with a plan for how to actually achieve them in a way where each person's needs are met and understood.'

It may be a case of trial and error when it comes to making sure both of you are happy with your intended path, but 'if someone says, "I want this and I'm not willing to negotiate", that's where you have an imbalance of power'.

Sometimes, the compromise is too great, though. It's perfectly acceptable to be unwilling to compromise on certain things that you desire, whether that's a safe home, children, or time spent working abroad. 'You need to decide on the things you're going to compromise on. If you're not willing to compromise on it, maybe it's not the right relationship for you,' Lucille advises.

Importantly, beware of compromising while believing that you can change your partner's mind in time. In the first year, someone might be on their best behaviour but over time, their true self will come to the fore. In that first year, be highly attuned to your compatibility levels. Don't ignore nagging concerns and hope that they'll change their mind later. For example, if you really want kids and your partner is telling you they don't, you've got to take them at their word, hard as that might be.

Lucille serves up some tough love: 'If you're turning a blind eye early on, and saying once they love me, they'll settle down, you're setting yourself up for disappointment. They're telling you; you're just not hearing it.

'If it's too big of a sacrifice where you feel like you will not be happy, then that's information. If you're not going to feel safe if you don't have a house and they're telling you we're not going to have that, that's information.'

Rising above resentment

Resentment kicks in when one person isn't getting their needs met at all. To avoid resentment, you need to be able to compromise. It should go without saying, you're headed for a rocky road if one, or both of you, are unwilling to meet in the middle.

In the event that you do get stuck in a difficult place and can't find a resolution that enables you to move towards a shared vision, Lucille says it's essential to frame *the issue* as the problem, not the other person. If you can approach the issue as a team, you're more likely to find a successful resolution. But if you're locking horns with each other over having your needs met, the conflict can become overwhelming. That's when you need to return to prioritising love and respect. Each couple must be able to respectively navigate between their personal objectives in life and their intertwined goals as 'us'. If you're able to do that, you can then decide, 'What are our priorities as a couple?'

Goal setting and shared vision

In the beginning, you'll start talking about your individual and shared goals to see if there are any substantial barriers to achieving them. At the same time, you'll be wanting to see if a shared future path is feasible. Goals and shared visions will naturally vary from couple to couple but it'll probably come up sooner than you expect it to, because you'll likely have had goals prior to meeting, and you may be eager to get your partner involved in your aspirations too.

For example, if your new lover wants to coax you into a year living in a bohemian commune while you've been squirrelling away funds for a lavish trip to Italy, that could be a strong sign that your short-term goals are misaligned. That said, if you're both equally excited by the prospect of saving for a few weeks in Thailand: bingo.

Lucille explains that discussing short, medium and long-term goals is actually an 'exploration of compatibility'. And as far as long-term visions go, there doesn't need to be a set timeframe. She believes it's best to see what feels right for your partnership as you grow together, so you might start with holidays and short-term planning for things you want to do together, then start thinking longer-term when you're comfortably established as a team.

But how do you work out what your shared vision is? What if you don't have a clear burning drive to live in another country for a year, own an art gallery or become activists? Lucille says, 'The vision doesn't need to be big. The vision might be a really connected loving relationship; it might be raising children.' The key is simply to create meaning together and want to support one another's dreams.

With a vision in place, you can look at the more granular aspects, the associated costs, the underlying values required and the impact on your relationship. If the long-term vision is to have a family, you'd likely want to discuss your shared values and how that shapes your parenting style. Regardless of what the vision is, though, Lucille says you also need to ask yourselves, 'How are we going to stay connected as a couple?' Because a shared vision is much harder to achieve if you put all of your energy into getting there and lose the love along the way.

Staying connected for the long-haul requires more than regular date nights. Bringing the right individual qualities to your partnership is also essential. Being aware of your strengths and weaknesses in these areas and working on the qualities that need improvement shows you're committed to the relationship's success. Some qualities I had hoped to find in a significant other included: emotional vulnerability, honesty, trust, empathy and compatibility. Every quality on that list can be applied to how you manage finances. These factors can also be the root of fights over money or help you to flourish.

Emotional vulnerability

It's one thing to have great banter over dinner, but feeling safe to be emotionally vulnerable is also essential. When Sam and I talk about money, we don't just discuss the dollars and cents tied to a given situation, we talk about the emotional response a goal might trigger. So, when we discuss dipping into our savings for a big expense, I'm open about the fear and anxiety that can cause me. When we've shared our experiences with debt, we've talked not just about the numbers but the shame and frustration that can come with that. It's not always easy to have these chats, as we discussed in chapter two, but the upside is that being vulnerable about your financial concerns is great for your enduring connection.

Honesty

I don't know anyone who wants a liar for a partner, but when it comes to our approach to managing cash, sometimes many of us are guilty of lying by omission. Ever bought an item of clothing and then hid it in the wardrobe until it magically appeared for an occasion because you didn't want your partner to know that you'd splashed out on an outfit? Played down how much you spent on a night out because it's easier than fighting about it later? Said you were okay with a big purchase when you really weren't? These can seem like small things in isolation, but if you're not being honest with yourself or your partner, it's worth stopping and asking yourself why. Small secret purchases might seem innocuous but could become a larger issue over time.

Trust

If you ask your partner to pick up groceries on the way home, do you trust that they'll do it? That might be an easy one to say yes to, but when it comes to financial decisions, the level of trust required is much higher. When Sam started putting funds into our home, his name wasn't on the mortgage. He trusted me to put the money he contributed into the mortgage and renovation, not to go out and blow it on a whim. Prior to him contributing financially, I trusted him to add value in our home in other ways and not to take advantage of me. That's not to say you should be naive and rely on trust alone, but there's a balance required. Without trust, you risk weakening your connection.

Empathy

I felt a great deal of shame when I had a lot of credit card debt and no savings. That's framed the way that I listen to other people's financial challenges. Perhaps you were raised in a family where money wasn't discussed at all, or significant consumer debt was an accepted part of life. It's possible that your partner has experienced financial abuse, struggled with unemployment or lost a large sum through a poor business decision. People aren't just naturally good or bad with money, their cumulative experiences drive their actions. I also don't believe you necessarily need to write someone off if they're not in a good financial position; the question is whether or not they're willing to do the work to improve so you can both commit to shared goals. A financial position is rarely just about the money you have or don't have; there's likely a lot of complex emotion tied to it, so approaching your plan with mutual financial empathy is vital if you want to enhance your position and maintain a strong relationship, too.

Compatibility

It's pretty easy to work out if you enjoy each other's company and whether you generally want the same lifestyle, but financial compatibility is a whole other thing. I don't know many couples who tackle their finances in the same way. One's a saver; one's the spender. Or one has a lot of anxiety attached to taking financial risks, while the other has no issue throwing money into cryptocurrency. I like to have enough money on hand to feel comfortable and I spend a lot of time looking to the future. This can be useful, but can also pull me out of enjoying the present. Sam has a happy-go-lucky mindset and doesn't worry so much about the future, but he's not reckless. He's better at having fun on a budget than I am. We are different when it comes to money management, but our differences are helping us to get better at our respective downfalls. Chances are both you and your partner will have financial strengths and weaknesses. Finding the common ground and being prepared to move forward together is essential.

Converting goals into a shared vision

Once you have your goal-setting groove and you're ready to discuss a shared vision, it's time to solidify the vision by asking one another specific questions and establishing how you'll convert your goals into a feasible shared vision. Individual goals such as starting a business, having kids, retiring early – whatever you aspire to – all add up to the shared vision for your future. As you achieve each goal, you're a step closer to living the vision you imagine.

You might ask your partner, 'If you want kids, when do you want them? If you want to get married, when do you want to do that? If you want to buy a house, how will we work together?'

With an aspirational year or date in mind, you can then ask yourselves, 'Is that timeframe realistic?' That's not to say you should be demanding a marriage proposal or expecting to have a precise date to start bidding on houses, but you can't plan without a generally agreed month, year or decade to work to.

Whatever your shared vision is, you don't want to set and forget. If your vision is to own your home in three years time, it's not enough to talk about it once. According to Lucille, 'It's good to have check-ins every month, six months or year and ask, "Where are we at with achieving that?"'

These check-ins should also integrate questions about your relationship, not just your goals and visions. This is because your shared aspirations won't be nearly as feasible if the pulse of your relationship stops.

Some of Lucille's clients do this once a month on a Sunday night. I can't help but feel this is a pretty mundane way for a couple to spend the last hours of their weekend, but she insists that you can still make it romantic. And she's right. Emotional vulnerability is sexy, and as we've discussed, intimate conversations strengthen your connection.

Plenty of people are put off by a rigid checklist, but that just means you need to find a way that works for you. If you'd rather be bingeing your latest series or having a bath, that's understandable, but heed the caution in Lucille's experience as a therapist: 'So many issues come from assumptions and filling the blanks. Pretending that you can read your partner's mind never works.'

So, if you really want to make your vision a reality, you've got to have these chats.

Sam and I both had a pretty good idea of what we valued most – for me it was security and flexibility. But sometimes there's tension between those two things, because for me flexibility means working on my terms. In the past, that has meant being self-employed and that comes with the risk of income fluctuations, which in turn threaten my security.

There have been several times in my life where I've put myself into questionable financial positions because I wanted the flexibility to be creative, and the stress of managing the erratic income eventually put me back into secure salaried roles – often at the expense of my personal aspirations.

In recent years, I've accepted that at this point in my financial life, I simply can't have the security of a home without consistent income, but that doesn't mean I have to give up on flexibility completely. I seek out employment that allows space in my days for creativity. Sam's big driver is flexibility and time for creativity, too. Though like me, he still prioritises his trade as his primary source of income. But as we worked to develop our long-term vision, we believed that if we were disciplined, we would be able to have both security and more flexibility in the years to come.

Outside of work, we like being able to sit on our back deck with a glass of wine before dinner and chat about the day we've had. We really value stretches of relaxing time. Right now, we don't have too many of those though – there's always work to do.

We both love the process of restoring old homes and have talked about perhaps renovating another property in the future, but in the short term, we know we need to take care of our own backyard – ideally get rid of our car loans and finish working on our home first. By talking through the priorities, we've been able to set some goals and align our values in a way that helps us get our act together now, putting us on a path to living our shared vision for the future.

Goal-setting strategy

Sam and I were both new to properly structuring financial goals that truly reflected our values, so we engaged financial planner Rebecca Pritchard to help us learn how to set our goals properly and then develop a strategy to execute them.

Step One: doing a goal-setting exercise

First, Rebecca got us to focus on our basic, comfortable and dream lifestyles. She suggested thinking of this like a healthy eating pyramid. At the bottom (basic lifestyle) we need all of the nutritious fundamentals and at the top (dream lifestyle) we ideally get to enjoy the sweet stuff. We completed the form separately, then came back together to finesse it until we were both happy.

I thought it would be fun because it was all hypothetical. But, surprisingly, working out the dream was harder than we expected it to be because this is not a 'winning the lotto' dream. It was a case of establishing what our ideal future looks like and what we need to adjust in our current financial position so that we can achieve our shared vision.

Here's a peek at some of the examples on it:

	Basic lifestyle	**Comfortable lifestyle**	**Dream lifestyle**
Short-term (the next three years)	• Be personal-debt free (including ending car finance) • Reduce amount owing on our mortgage	• Finish basic renovation work • New kitchen	• An international holiday • Completely finished renovation and landscaped garden • Building a share portfolio
Mid-term (three – ten years)	• Continue to reduce the mortgage • One annual holiday	• Building a share portfolio • Buy an investment property	• Nic and Sam in a position to reduce day job hours and derive income from self-employment on our terms

	Basic lifestyle	Comfortable lifestyle	Dream lifestyle
Long-term (ten years from now to retirement)	• Nic and Sam in a position to reduce day job hours and derive income from self-employment on our terms	• Mortgage free on our Ballarat home	• Nic and Sam working only by choice and travelling in between
Retirement	• Mortgage free on our Ballarat home • $60,000 passive income	• Mortgage free + $80,000 passive income • One holiday per year	• Mortgage free + $100,000 passive income • Regular travel

Step Two: Dissecting our goals

When we reviewed our goals assignment with Rebecca, I'd hoped she'd simply tell us what we needed to do to make the goals in these boxes a reality. She works with couples to really understand their dynamic and their specific needs so she can perform her role as a financial planner. What ensued was more like couples counselling than financial advice – and that was a good thing.

When there's a professional in the mix, guiding the conversation, you'll hear your partner differently.

We both admitted the process had been harder than we'd expected it to be. For Sam, that was because he's never been one to plan too far into the future. For me, it was because every time I'd set a big goal, it had been quite confronting. This was because often there was a significant risk attached to the goal, particularly my most recent leap in moving to Ballarat on my own. I was now largely where I wanted to be, so the exercise made me think more about how I wanted to spend my days. Now that I'd achieved my long-held goal of buying a freestanding home and had settled down with Sam, our future together really required more consideration and discussion.

Rebecca challenged some of the stuff in our boxes. I'd put things like 'buy an investment property' in a box because I thought that was something we *should* do. But I couldn't back up the 'should' with a strong reason why or apply a clear value. Similarly, I'd added travel because who doesn't want regular trips to exotic locations? But it wasn't actually something either of us were yearning for at all.

As part of the process, we also considered where we wanted to be in six months time and what we wanted to see and feel that was different to the present moment. At this point, Sam was exploring the possibility of working more for himself, so his immediate goal was consistent income and a good rhythm to his weeks. I wanted to stop obsessing about interest rates and automate more of our banking, so I wasn't spending so much mental energy on what came in and went out.

It turns out that the exercise was designed simply to get us thinking about what we really wanted, and to have a more considered conversation about it. Some of the stuff we'd written down – such as international travel – was 'noise'. I know that plenty of people value travel and that's understandable, we definitely wanted a holiday at some point but Sam and I had both had our share of adventures, so travel wasn't as important to us as, say, fixing our crumbling kitchen. And when we distilled what we wanted further, it was really simple in the short term: clear our car loans, finish our renovation and improve our financial administration so that we knew how hard we actually needed to work.

This would alleviate much of my anxiety about security and put us on a path to more flexibility – flexibility that wouldn't be risky like it had for me in the past, because we'd have all of the financial foundations firmly in place.

As part of this exercise, we also gave Rebecca access to our full financial picture: savings accounts, superannuation, the mortgage and our expenses. I fully expected her to yell at us. Giving her an itemised diary of our spending made me feel vulnerable. Like, who were we to have big goals when we were regularly blowing money at the pub, ordering more UberEats than we should and paying off two financed cars?

'You know there are things you can do better,' she said. 'You didn't come in today expecting me to say "Guys, don't change anything."' What we needed to think about was what we might change in our lifestyle to 'live sustainably'. But Rebecca also said that if we were going to find more money to work towards our goals, we had to be intrinsically motivated. 'It's not a binge diet; it's something healthy that you carry forward,' she said.

On the upside, she told us we already had a few runs on the board financially, emotionally and behaviourally, and it was Sam who reminded me that we'd actually done a lot of positive financial work in our first year together, setting up a savings habit and adding value to our home as we renovated. Plus, we talked openly and vulnerably which was just as important as doing the money work.

It was psychologically compelling to put our goals under a microscope: I was really self-critical; Sam was far more positive about our progress. And this likely came back to our key values: mine being security above all else, and I didn't feel like we were there yet. But what is *there*? For me it's knowing that the mortgage on the house is a comfortable sum, and we're never in a position where a surprise expense becomes a problem. The process of working things through with our financial planner was practical and enlightening. It enabled us to really dig deep into our values and aspirations and see the path ahead.

Couple goals check-in

There's lots to digest here, but if you take away one thing it's the exercise in working out your basic, comfortable and dream lifestyle goals, because working out those goals – particularly the long-term objectives – may help you to crystallise your vision. I encourage you to try it yourself – both individually and together – then ask yourself these questions:

- Have we discussed our individual and shared values?
- Do any of our values cause conflict? If so, where can we compromise?
- What do our basic, comfortable and dream lifestyles look like?
- Do we need to implement any lifestyle changes to make our long-term vision a reality?

CHAPTER SIX

Cashflow for couples

As motivating as the conversation with Rebecca Pritchard was, I couldn't see how we were going to get to a point where I wasn't worried about the damn mortgage and car repayments. I couldn't see beyond simply making sure all of our financial obligations were met each month, let alone being able to do this comfortably. All I knew at this point was that of my monthly salary, there was very little left in the days before my next pay arrived. While we did have some savings on hand, we weren't adding much to them, so I felt that we were still treading water.

That's because we didn't have a shared cashflow plan, which was in part because we were still operating a lot of our finances separately.

According to Rebecca, 'It's important to understand the lay of the land, particularly in an environment where you're living together. At that point you've got to call a spade a spade.

You have shared expenses. Irrespective of how you've decided to pay for those expenses, they are shared.' This meant it was time for us to transition beyond managing our finances from a mostly individual perspective and come together more effectively as a team.

We needed to look seriously at what our lifestyle was costing us in total, regardless of who was bringing in the money. Rebecca told us that while it can be confronting to face poor habits, it's also 'incredibly powerful to understand your expenses, which in turn helps you to get organised with your money so you can reach your goals. Then you know when you can take your foot off the pedal.'

I knew she was right. Up until this point Sam and I had both been fighting our individual financial fires and getting ahead was all 'finger in the air' kind of stuff. Like, maybe we could clear our car finance in a year or two if we were disciplined. Maybe we could be chipping away at more than the minimum mortgage repayments. Maybe we could find more money to invest. But we didn't have a proper set of priorities or a strategy to execute them, and we couldn't form one without a clear picture of our total income and expenditure. We needed to look at our shared household costs so we could see what was coming in; what was going out; all the nitty-gritty. So, now, we're going to get granular with cashflow.

Collective cashflow

The thing about cashflow for couples is that you can't structure it properly unless you're prepared to be completely transparent about absolutely everything you earn and spend. Cashflow is confronting because you have to sit down and ask yourself if you really need to buy two coffees a day or why you've been paying for a gym membership that you haven't used for six months. Is having a car under finance slowing down your financial progress? These can be tough questions to tackle together.

It's also difficult if you're used to having your own bank account and haven't had to explain purchases to a partner. Improving your cashflow doesn't necessarily mean you need a joint bank account if that's not right for your circumstances, but you do need to be candid about your income and spending so you can work out precisely how much you have to put towards shared goals.

Transparency

In the early months of our relationship, Sam and I were taking each other mostly at our word. We weren't privy to each other's accounts, but as our relationship developed, it became clear we were going to need to physically see at least some of each other's numbers. So we set up a shared drive and started filing everything that we both needed access to; if not at that moment, perhaps later for tax or other purposes. This was extremely handy when it came time to complete our cashflow exercise.

You might file things differently to us depending on your circumstances, but here are the folders we've set up:

Bank statements – I file bank statements so that I can refer back to them for a high-level view of where our money is going.

Bills – because I had the house before Sam came along, most of the bills come to me. I file them so that we have an accessible record of our water, gas, electricity, council rates and internet.

Cars – in this folder we put anything related to our vehicles which includes any car finance information, car insurance, rego receipts and log books.

House – here I've saved everything related to the property including the property title, renovation and home and contents insurance in case we need to refer to it.

Insurance – this folder is home to all relevant health and life insurance policies.

Legal – this is where we hold anything related to the management of our assets. Wills and estate planning documents also go here.

Shares – I have an extremely modest share portfolio. I keep the associated admin documents here.

Super – I save both of our annual statements in this folder.

I don't keep anything from Sam. He can look at any statement he likes. But I'd never itemised my spending and handed it to him. Probably because he'd be mortified to see some of my 'discretionary spending' – particularly in terms of things such as skincare, hair appointments and contact lenses. Also, wine. I knew I was spending far too much on my favourite vice. But if I was going to ask this of him, I had to get vulnerable about my healthy and unhealthy habits.

Creating your cashflow

In early 2023, when we started our formal financial planning process, interest rates were rising steadily, the mortgage alone was more than $3,000 per month, and we also had two cars under finance. After petrol, bills and general living expenses, we rarely had much left to put into savings – at least, that's what we believed. We didn't consider our lifestyle to be extravagant or reckless, but we did often live in the moment and spend spontaneously. Deep down we knew that if we were more intentional with our income, we'd definitely be able to save more each month.

So is there an optimal way for couples to manage their budget and cashflow if they want to reach their financial goals? Rebecca uses the word 'cashflow' rather than budget, because budget has restrictive and limiting connotations. 'Cashflow', on the other hand, is a far more optimistic description. 'Cashflow' provides a good visual breakdown of income and spending, and helps couples to see how their money can be used to live sustainably (rather than pay cheque to pay cheque).

To understand your shared cashflow, first you'll need to calculate your shared income and deduct all of your expenses, which will, hopefully, leave you with a surplus.

In terms of how money is divided up each month, Rebecca says there are still 'values conversations' to be had. For example, how much is reasonable to spend on groceries and dining? You might value quality food, whereas your partner might be happy with a no-frills diet, so there's some spending balance required in that case.

Once you've established what is essential (rent/mortgage repayments, bills and so on), and you turn your attention to discretionary spending (food, entertainment, personal needs), whatever money is left over can be put into savings, investments and your specific goals.

If there's not enough at the bottom of your cashflow to help you work towards your goals in a suitable timeframe, the question to ask is: Where can we make adjustments?

You don't need a financial planner to give you a sophisticated document to list everything you're earning and spending; you can do this at home. Just open a spreadsheet and list relevant items in the following categories to tally your numbers.

When you're looking at your overall cashflow and how it's managed, here are some things to consider:

Income

Your income is any amount of money that lands in either of your bank accounts which includes salaries, any additional funds made through bonuses, side hustles and freelance work (less any associated tax). It may also include dividends from shares and any gains on savings accounts that generate interest.

Your income may also include any retirement benefits such as the age pension and social-security payments. In summary, your income is:

- Both of your salaries (before tax, excluding super)
- Bonuses
- Other taxable income (investment property rental income, dividends, side hustles)
- Retirement income or government payments.

Once you have all of your income calculated, you will need to deduct any associated tax. For example, if you sell any assets such as property or shares and make a profit, the money made is taxable income. But how do you calculate how much your taxable income will be?

Establishing your tax needs

I consulted with accountant and tax agent Julian Mauro to find out how tax can impact your cashflow. He recognises that both individuals and couples need financial processes that reflect their present lifestyle and their long-term goals. The way couples manage money is hugely dependent on what they're setting out to achieve.

The way you file important documents will depend on your current position. Considerations include whether you have an investment property or shares and whether one of you, or both of you, are self-employed. From there, you can establish a checklist that will help you stay on track. There are no hard and fast rules when it comes to filing, but this is particularly important if you're self-employed or generating additional side income because you'll need to account for any tax and GST.

Whatever's needed for your circumstances, Julian does suggest filing key documents as you go, keeping them in a digital folder, so at tax time it doesn't require you rifling back through the past year's paperwork.

He also recommends spending time monthly going through everything together, at which point you can review your projected tax if you're self-employed or have a side hustle and see how you're tracking with your goals.

If you do need to put money aside for tax and don't have a formal company set up, you may be unsure how much tax you'll need to pay. It can also be complex if you have a job with a salary and make additional income on top of that.

If you or your partner aren't sure how much you're likely to make in a given financial year, try using a digital service such as Pay Calculator (paycalc.com.au) which will give you a sense of how much you're each likely to earn and what the associated tax might be.

However, if you're a sole trader, or you have a job and a side hustle or freelance income, there might be some forecasting and estimating on your part. Keeping ongoing financial records and staying up to date is the best way to enable accurate forecasting. According to Julian, 'If you don't have historical data, you're guessing.'

In the event that you do need to put income aside for any tax and GST, Julian advocates for putting more aside than you need to if you can: 'If you put away too much, you can take it back.'

Once you know how much you're paying in additional tax, if any, you can more accurately calculate how much you're bringing in together.

Expenses

Your expenses are the outgoings associated with the general cost of living and also your lifestyle. This includes food, transport, pets, travel and general social life expenses. They can fluctuate depending on the time of year. Occasions during which you might splash out such as birthdays and holidays may alter your expenses from one month to the next. But ideally, when you have a cashflow strategy, you'll be taking portions of your surplus and putting them aside, so that you have funds on hand for those events.

We calculated our exact monthly expenses in retrospect. As tedious as it was, we went back over all of our bank statements and added every single transaction to our spreadsheet from coffees to cat food. That way, we were able to see a precise reflection of what we spent to give us an estimate of what an average year might look like. Some examples of expenses include:

- Groceries
- Socialising and entertainment
- Clothes
- Subscriptions
- Gifts
- Petrol/public transport
- Pet food and vet visits
- Childcare or school fees
- Utilities (gas, water, electricity)
- Council rates
- Phone and internet
- Vehicle registration and maintenance
- Home maintenance
- Insurance
- Gym memberships
- Donations
- Work and educational expenses

Repayments, savings and investments

Repayments are the non-negotiable expenses that you're required to pay on time. These are costs that require a level of accountability and result in consequences if you don't meet your obligations, i.e. if you don't pay your mortgage or car loan, you're going to be in strife. Here you'll also include your savings and investments (money that comes out of your income to go into a savings buffer or investment portfolio that you're building).

- Mortgage repayments
- Car loans
- Savings
- Investments

Your cashflow

The key is to work out your total income as a couple and deduct your outgoings so that you can see what's left. Here's a simple example:

Let's say one of you earns $80,000 per year, and the other earns $60,000 per year. It's possible that you will be able to make claims on work expenses which will reduce your taxable income, but for the purpose of this exercise, we'll assume you're not making any claims and therefore have no tax offsets. Additionally, we're assuming you have no student debt.

Associated tax deductions:

Person one income: $80,000 per year

Year 2022–2023	Annually
Gross income (excluding super)	$80,000.00
Tax	$16,467.00
Medicare levy	$1,600.00
Net income	**$61,933.00**

Person two income: $60,000 per year

Year 2022–2023	Annually
Gross income (excluding super)	$60,000.00
Tax	$9,967.00
Medicare levy	$1,200.00
Net income	**$48,933.00**

Net income as a couple (excluding any tax returns):

Person one: $61,933

Person two: $48,933

Total: $110,866

Expenses

Like income, I've kept your expenses reasonably simple. Here I've assumed that you have a mortgage and therefore you pay council rates, and at this time you don't have children therefore you don't have childcare or school fees to pay. You don't have any pets or a gym membership. You share one car. You have couples' private health insurance, but you don't currently have a life insurance policy or other protection. The monthly figures are for both of your expenses combined.

Expense	Amount per month	Annual total
Groceries	$1,000	$12,000
Socialising and entertainment	$1,000	$12,000
Clothes	$200	$4,800
Personal (hair, beauty products)	$150	$1,800
Subscriptions	$40	$480
Gifts	$100	$1,200
Petrol/public transport	$600	$7,200
Utilities (gas, water, electricity)	$500	$6,000
Council rates	$180	$2,160
Phone and internet	$200	$4,800
Vehicle registration and maintenance	$120	$1,440
Home maintenance	$170	$2,040
Insurance	$250	$3,000
TOTAL		$58,920

Repayments, savings and investments

Here I have assumed that you have a monthly mortgage repayment (but this can be replaced with a rental figure if you're renting). The car you share is under finance, you're contributing a small amount to savings each month, but you're not currently investing.

Repayment	Amount per month	Annual total
Mortgage	$3,000	$36,000
Car loan	$450	$5,400
Savings	$400	$4,800
TOTAL		**$46,200**

Now that you know the total you bring in together and the total that's likely to be spent over the course of the year, you have a shared cashflow and a remaining surplus.

Cashflow	Annual total
Income after tax	$110,866
Total expenses	-$58,920
Total repayments, savings and investments	-$46,200
TOTAL SURPLUS	**$5,746**

So, as you can see, you have almost $6,000 left to put towards your goals. Perhaps you put more into savings and investments. Maybe you're hit with an unexpected bill, and it comes out of your leftover funds. How you divvy it up will depend on the stage you're at in your relationship and what you're working towards. Importantly, reviewing your cashflow will help you to look at where you're spending unnecessarily. If you'd like to save an additional $10,000 per year rather than $6,000, where can you cut costs or grow income to find that extra $4,000?

We're not just doing this exercise to work out a potential surplus; it's also a tool to help you see how powerful you are together, regardless of individual income. Few couples are likely to bring in exactly the same amount each. One of you will probably earn more than the other. In some cases one of you might earn significantly more, or perhaps someone's on parental leave. There could be any number of reasons why there's income disparity between you, but when you look at your combined income holistically, you might find that you're able to achieve more working as a team than you do individually.

How do you manage cashflow when one person earns more than the other?

There are so many scenarios that could dictate the way that you decide which portions of your income are allocated to shared expenses, but at a minimum, it should be as transparent as required in your circumstances, and the set up should also be fair for both of you. Regardless of how you split the finances in your household based on who earns what, there are some things you can do to strengthen your holistic approach to maximising your incomes together.

Rebecca says that the priority in any relationship should be to work out what's fair. That's because a 50/50 split of every cost may be equal, but that doesn't necessarily make it fair in your specific circumstances. It could also slow down your big picture progress.

So, what is fair? The best outcome likely requires a mindset shift, in which you focus less on who earns what, and more on the goals you've put on the table: 'You need to say to each other, "We have *us* goals, *me* goals and *you* goals – what are we focusing on?"'

In her work, Rebecca has found that those who do well in goal setting and execution leave individual incomes out of the equation. 'Breadwinner is a term that only exists in solo income households. It doesn't make sense in a household where two people are earning, even if there is a discrepancy in earning.'

What matters is that each person is contributing the most that they can to their present life together and their future aspirations. Not just financially, but in all aspects of the relationship, from household labour to showing up for the other person. Each member of the partnership should be able to say, 'I'm working as hard as I can with whatever I have to bring to the table and you're doing the same. We're happy and that's fair.'

Broadly, Rebecca advocates for couples to look at their earnings as a total amount, because when funds aren't mostly shared between a couple, imbalances are activated, both financially and emotionally. Problems arise when one person is inclined to overspend and the other isn't, or goals are skewed in one person's favour.

However, as nice as it is to say that it doesn't matter who earns what, it's not always that simple, and often gender still plays a key part in this. According to Rebecca, 'The more common situation is for women to be the lower income earners. If they are trying to keep up, they may feel like they are failing, because they're not contributing as much financially.'

By contrast, research indicates when a woman is the higher income earner, 'her share of domestic duties goes up – it's compensating. They say they'll do the saving and investing, which in turn can also lead to not having a comfortable standard of living.'

That's in fact why you might consider being mostly 'all in' with a partner and treating money like 'ours' rather than yours and mine. I say 'mostly' because as we explored earlier, some personal autonomy is still valuable, but an agreed structure that celebrates both contributions may actually reduce any sense of earning inequality.

For your cashflow plan to work, you need a clear picture of your shared financial health, which relies on both of you being completely transparent and consistently engaged in what happens with your household spending.

Pay your goals together

Sam and I see our income as a total amount for us to work with and we don't believe it matters who generates what. It only matters that we work the figures to our advantage. At various junctures in our life together, the person earning more will likely change, and perhaps at times one of us will not be drawing an income at all. The percentage of each contribution is a distraction from what should be the main focus: we have a stronger ability to save and invest as a team than either of us ever did on our own.

According to financial advisor Jess Brady, being clear on your values will help you to start reviewing how you live now in terms of the way you spend your money and whether you have alignment between your values and your spending in a practical sense. Understanding what you want your days to look like now and into your future will help to form the financial aspects of your goals.

As I mentioned, Sam and I went through the process of putting our goals into phases, from the immediate future right through to retirement. Jess advocates for a similar approach, looking at the short, medium and long-term.

Once you have shared objectives for each phase of time, she says you need to work out what the 'must dos' are and be prepared for trade-offs with your non-essential goals. So, for example, starting a business or buying a house might be a non-negotiable, while a goal to take an international holiday is put on the backburner. Then, establish how much each goal is going to cost and cross-check your cashflow to make sure you have the savings to fund the plan. Jess also recommends automating your banking so that you're allocating funds to your goals without question every time you're paid.

Automating your cashflow

Once you've completed your cashflow, you'll be well placed to automate your personal banking. I have historically been terrible at this. Until recently, I was still manually paying my phone bill and other costs that came in. But with a clear cashflow plan, Sam and I were equipped to work out which portions of our income we could syphon off to be better prepared for upcoming costs. We arranged direct transfers of funds so that bills were paid on time automatically, and direct transfers were made into our goal funds as soon as we were paid, so that there was no temptation to spend elsewhere.

If you're serious about achieving your goals, you need to treat regular surplus deposits towards your goals as non-negotiable. That means automating your payments and ensuring you don't dip into these funds to make other purchases because, as Jess points out, 'leaving your goal to take what's left at the end of the pay cycle will mean it will likely starve. It should be paid straight after you get paid and you should have enough buffer to not take it out.'

Aside from anything else, automation reduced the amount of time Sam and I spend on administration. Funds simply zoom off to the places they needed to go: mortgage, bills, savings, personal spending, goals and so on; all the money goes into the respective accounts as instructed. I'll show you exactly how our cashflow is broken down and distributed to our goals later.

Couple goals check-in

Cashflow can be confronting if you're not used to being explicit about your spending and earnings with your partner. Here are some things to sit down together and discuss at this check-in:

- Do we know how much we bring in as a team now?
- How much money will our jobs generate in the coming years?
- Rather than focusing on who earns what, how can we use our total income to achieve more together?
- Do we need to automate more of our bills, savings and goal targets?
- Are we both sharing the mental load of the administration and any stressors associated with our position?
- Where can we improve our cashflow? Are we spending too much in one area?

CHAPTER SEVEN

Protecting your assets

At the beginning of a relationship, when you're riding high on pheromones, you're probably not all that enthusiastic about the terribly mundane matter of asset protection. And you're unlikely to be entertaining the reality of losing some or all of an asset to this person, who right now is the centre of your universe. But when things get serious, you'll need to put your sensible hat back on. Before you found love, you were probably living a successful single life. Maybe you had your own business, you'd hustled to buy a home on your own, got into investing or you've just been smart with your money and have a pot of savings to your name. No matter how big or small your asset pool is, you need to know how being in a relationship can impact your assets. So, let's look at some asset types and what happens to them when you couple up.

When one person owns a business

There are more than 2.5 million businesses operating in Australia, and the vast majority – approximately 98 per cent – were small to medium enterprises (SMEs). That's a lot of sole traders and people employing less than twenty people.

Australians love having a professional punt. Whether that's opening a cafe, choosing to go out on your own as a self-employed tradie or working as a freelance consultant, we're increasingly sticking our necks out to take control of our financial futures.

But that can have significant financial and emotional implications. The question is: Can your relationship withstand the stress of having your own business – or any significant financial leap of faith?

CASE STUDY

Nobody wants to be a financial liability in their relationship, but this was a risk Owen Raszkiewicz had to take. He had a vision for a business, one that his partner was prepared to support both emotionally and financially.

The pair have been together since they were teenagers. Now aged thirty-three, Owen hosts *The Australian Finance Podcast* with co-host Kate Campbell. He's qualified in financial planning, and he owns an investment and financial education platform.

Given Owen's professional finance background coupled with his long-term relationship, I assumed he'd be one of the best people to speak with about managing money as a duo, but even Owen and his partner have faced challenges.

'Most of our money journey was simple; we were a team,' Owen says, although he adds that this was a double-edged sword because their financial position was enmeshed from the get-go. 'You don't get a chance to think about your own finances because you're young,' he says.

For the bulk of their relationship, everything was shared – joint bank accounts ensured they could see their income and outgoings. 'Traditionally budgeting was in my partner's court and investing was in mine,' he says.

They had their system and knew their strengths. 'I had an informational advantage, but she had a behavioural advantage – she's very cool, calm and collected with money.' It worked for them, but that doesn't mean that they were talking about it. In fact, Owen admits, 'I had my head in the sand. I had a lot of insecurities regarding managing money, which comes from my parents. She was much more stable in terms of talking about money as a family.'

'I tended to shut down when talking about money unless it was the investing side. I knew there were things that you should do and not do, but I didn't want to talk about it,' he says. This surprised me, but as Owen points out, this has been our societal set-up until recently. Males were hunter-gatherers and women managed the household. The age-old gender split ensured there was nothing to discuss. But of course, 'that's changing rapidly,' Owen says.

Their arrangement is far from traditional. In his twenties, Owen had enough in savings to purchase a home, but instead he put the money he had into starting his business. For four years he didn't earn a stable income and they lived mostly off his partner's wage. They were making significant financial decisions together, so why was it so hard for Owen to talk about? 'In my opinion, when you put everything on the table, you're laid bare – your vulnerabilities are exposed,' he says.

In recent years, Owen has addressed his experiences with a psychologist and is now much better at discussing finances with his partner. An important part of that evolution has actually involved giving themselves more independence and ensuring they have individual goals as well as shared objectives. As a result, they now have their own personal bank accounts and personal budgets as well as their shared funds. It means if they want to save up and buy something that's important to them, they can. No questions asked.

'Having some money of your own is good for your wellbeing,' Owen says. 'In the past, when everything was mingled, if I wanted to do something, I felt like I was being selfish. Having met so young, it was important that we became individuals.' Although Owen says, 'I'm not going to do anything crazy without consulting her.'

When it comes to larger financial decisions, Owen says that while money is obviously a factor, these decisions are actually about lifestyle and goals. 'The biggest issue is where our goals don't overlap; it then leads to the trade-off. Then we have to prioritise whose goal comes first. That's relationship 101.'

There's not always an easy answer, though. 'I want to do Everest base camp, and that's not something my partner is interested in. She wants to go to Europe. We haven't got to the bottom of that one, but that's where budgeting ourselves helps,' Owen says.

But on the whole, they operate with complete transparency. They have no debt other than their mortgage. 'We have access to each other's bank accounts, and we pay bills as one unit.' Asset-wise there are some clear distinctions. Their home is in Owen's partner's name because he is the sole director and owner of the business. If he was ever to get sued, the home is protected because it's not in his name. This is not uncommon. Many people who operate a small business will give themselves this layer of security.

In other areas, Owen's partner has more superannuation than he does because she has been working in a salaried role, while he spent time building his business. That said, he has been more focused on investing. Owen has also encouraged her to consider more investments as part of her personal budget.

The way they've worked together is pretty extraordinary. It takes a rock-solid relationship to withstand four years of sacrifice and financial instability. Not to mention some serious setbacks in which Owen had to let staff go and borrow significant sums to keep going.

Fortunately, it paid off. In late 2022, Owen hosted a candid solo podcast in which he told his audience the business is now worth a million dollars and is on track to keep growing.

They're clearly doing well together, but what happens if they were ever to split up? 'We talk about this a lot – we'd take most of what is in our names. My partner would take most of the house and I would take most of the business.'

Tax for self-employed couples

If you do own a business or are considering starting one, the structure can also have tax implications. The way you're taxed will depend on whether you set up a company, become a sole trader or run the business through a trust.

For example, someone might make $120,000 as a salary and an additional $30,000 in side hustle income as a sole trader (this means they have an ABN, but don't have a formal company set up), bringing their total income to $150,000. That person will likely be paying more than 30 per cent in tax on the additional $30,000 that they've earned.

Company structures are different and according to Owen, 'Any money that you don't take out of the company bank account is called retained earnings. They're taxed at 25 per cent instead of the marginal tax rates that we pay as an individual.'

'That means a company has a flat rate of tax, [so] whether you make $10,000 or a million bucks, it's still 25 per cent,' Owen says. Alternatively, sole traders – whether they spend the $30,000 or not – are going to pay 30 per cent tax on it. But, if the sole trader's income shot up to $250,000 they might be paying approximately 40 per cent tax on business income, versus 25 per cent as a company.

Asset imbalances

Whether the asset is owned prior to the relationship or secured during, Owen suggests that a willingness to engage in a conversation where one person asserts their need to protect their financial position is really the bare minimum.

You're within your right to draw up an agreement regarding 'anything where your risk is exposed'.

If you say, 'I need to protect myself and this is really important to me,' and there's resistance to that, then that's a serious red flag. Owen believes that a binding financial agreement or pre-nup should be put in place 'if someone comes to the relationship with assets and the other has nothing'. Over time, however, the protection will become less meaningful. Initially it's there to protect the person who has come to the relationship with more, but as the years pass, circumstances will change as you will work together to build wealth and the initial agreement will no longer be relevant.

Binding financial agreements

CASE STUDY

Back in 2007, when young people met on MySpace, Amy started chatting with her future husband, Jono. They eventually met in person at a nightclub in Sydney's Kings Cross. Amy recalls Jono approaching her and saying he was 'Jono from MySpace'. Amy played it cool. 'I was very coy, but I knew exactly who he was,' she says.

And that was the beginning of their life together. They spent a decade together before marrying in 2018.

At the same time they were enjoying life as a married couple, Jono's profile as a celebrity trainer was building and they were also plotting the launch of their premium personal training and fitness space.

'It always made sense for him to have his own space and his own brand,' Amy says. 'That's where I come in.' With a background in commerce and accounting, Amy took the lead on the financial aspects of setting up and running the business, along with sales, marketing and brand strategy.

They opened during Covid lockdowns in 2020. 'We were allowed to have a space that wasn't open to the public, and one-on-one training was allowed,' Amy explains. It was a risky time to launch a business, but they firmly believed in what they could achieve together – with or without a pandemic testing their resolve. 'We were joint partners from the start,' Amy says.

Amy believes it was their strong foundation as romantic partners that enabled them to set up a business as a married couple. 'I fully trust what he wants to put out there, what he wants to teach our staff and the way he trains. He trusts me in the direction that I see the brand going in,' she says.

Although, while they did make time for their relationship outside of working hours, 'There was no time we didn't work on the business. That was our passion,' Amy says. But they were also under a fair bit of pressure, operating a new business while 'adapting quickly to changing laws' as they moved in and out of lockdowns in 2020 and 2021. By the end of the long Sydney lockdown in 2021, they had decided to end their marriage, but maintain their business pursuits together.

In the early stages of their separation, Jono went to Los Angeles for three months. 'I was here holding the fort. It was a great opportunity for us to get some space away from each other. He came back with a different mindset,' Amy says. So, despite their separation, they wanted to keep their professional partnership alive. 'Jono and I agree there's no one else in the world that we would do this with.'

Continuing to run a business with a former spouse is not for everyone, but Amy and Jono show that it's possible if you have the emotional maturity and commitment to see through a shared goal. 'We did have contracts in place in terms of our business agreement and that stipulated our roles and responsibilities for the business. It was clear, there was no confusion as Jono and I own it 50/50,' Amy says. They also had several conversations with their accountant regarding the practical operation of the gym post-split.

A contractual agreement is one thing, but navigating the emotional impact is something else.

'It took about a year for us to get to the point that we're at now, and it's still evolving. Contracts and agreements state so much, but a massive part is that we still have respect and trust for each other,' Amy says.

The division of work was clear. Jono continued in his role as head trainer and Amy oversees operations and manages the brand's growth, along with additional staff that they've since hired to support her. Their personal lives became completely personal, and they agreed not to discuss who they were seeing, unless it was serious. 'We were not going out and being spiteful. We didn't need to do that to each other.'

'The only time I mentioned a new partner was my current partner, Aaron,' Amy says. Similarly, Jono didn't mention a new girlfriend until he formed a relationship with his partner, Simone. 'We all get along,' Amy says.

It might be unconventional, but Amy describes them as 'the Castano modern family'. It works, and they plan to run their business together long-term.

When there is net worth in the form of assets that one person has held prior to entering a relationship, financial advisor Jess Brady says a couple should ask themselves, 'How are we going to protect it?' Note here the emphasis is on *we*. In a good partnership, both parties should seek to protect an asset, even when it belongs to only one person. This is an important point. If your partner doesn't respect your need to look after something you've earned on your own, that may well be a warning sign.

A binding financial agreement isn't about keeping something valuable from a spouse, it's saying 'we love each other and we're connected', but also that an individual has the right to look after their financial future.

Family lawyer Perpetua Kish (who also goes by Pepe) says it is important to set rules for pre-existing assets when entering into a relationship, whether it be a marriage or a de facto relationship

So at what point is a couple exiting a relationship entitled to make a claim on assets? For example, I bought my property prior to meeting Sam. At what point could he make a claim on the house? Well, there have to be certain circumstances. A relationship is considered de facto if it has lasted at least two years. But having said that, claims can be made in relationships under two years depending what has happened during that time.

Beyond the length of the relationship, factors to consider are the nature of the relationship and its 'public reputation', the level of financial dependence and interdependence between the partners, and other relevant circumstances. For example, if Sam and I had a child or if a separation caused one of us a 'substantial injustice'.

What constitutes a substantial injustice? Well, let's say I had the house and had $100,000 owing on the mortgage. Sam comes in and pays off that $100,000 mortgage, but the house is still only in my name. According to Pepe Kish, it may be unjust for me to say to Sam, 'You have no right to my house.'

That sounds fair, as having him pay it off and then trying to claim it as my own is pretty unjust. Pepe says in such a situation, Sam may have a 'compelling action' under the *Family Law Act* if I refused to work with him and consider his contribution to the house if we called off our relationship.

But there are several factors that would determine a specific outcome. The reality is though that if someone gave you $100,000 for a property a few weeks before you split up, you'd probably have a strong argument to have that money paid back. But that changes the longer you're together. If that $100,000 was spent twenty years ago, it may no longer be relevant in the grand scheme of your relationship.

Conversely, in a marriage you are automatically considered to be in a relationship so that means the division of assets would be determined under the *Family Law Act*. But in a de facto relationship it's a little bit more complex. Let's say that the house remains in my name and Sam does pay off the $100,000, but then over the course of our relationship we go on to buy two additional investment properties, but we're still not married. What then?

Well, it all gets a bit complicated and would depend on many aspects in the relationship.

These factors can be all sorts of things including who earns more, who takes on care-giving responsibilities for children and the duration of the partnership. Pepe points out, 'It's certainly not a straight 50/50 split. This is one of the greatest myths in family law.'

To determine what is fair, a good example can be to think of the situation like the start of a running race. For the person who's deemed more vulnerable 'that might be the equivalent of running without shoes,' Pepe explains, so they're given something that gives them a fair start when the relationship ends.

The start of the race is just the beginning. One partner might encounter more difficulties that slow them down. Things such as earning a lower income or doing the childcare. The other person might have advantages, that in contrast, give them a competitive edge, such as more superannuation. 'Or they might be younger and have more years to work and earn income, or, they have a higher income or earning capacity,' she adds.

But depending on your circumstances, whether that be protecting something that was yours before the relationship started, or looking after children from a previous relationship, a binding financial agreement or a pre-nup can be drawn up. According to Pepe, 'They serve to oust the jurisdiction of the court, which means to remove or limit the power of the court to hear the case. With a binding financial agreement, you can reach a private agreement on any terms you seek, outside the court's scrutiny. If that is properly prepared, the parties can divide assets in any manner they wish, without needing to submit the agreement to the court to determine whether the proposed agreement is just and equitable.'

If you want your agreement to be legitimately binding, these documents must be drawn up by a lawyer, and each of you must have your own lawyer who provides independent legal advice.

You've got to do it properly. In the best case, Kish says a strong binding financial agreement will 'tell the story of your relationship, as this can provide narrative of the intention behind it'.

There are a number of things required to make your agreement a legally binding, enforceable document. Crucially both individuals need to get independent financial advice, not least because with money and assets, there is often associated power. Case in point: Thorne v Kennedy (Ms Thorne and Mr Kennedy are pseudonyms used to protect their identities).

Here's what happened: Ms Thorne was represented by family lawyer Peter Carmont after her husband, Mr Kennedy, who had assets valued between $18–$24 million, left her with only a small sum in the divorce. The pair met online in 2006 on a website that advertised potential brides.

Ms Thorne, who was then thirty-six, came to Australia from Eastern Europe to marry Mr Kennedy, sixty-seven.

Just days before they were due to wed, Mr Kennedy took Ms Thorne to a solicitor so that she could get legal advice on their binding financial agreement. There, she was told that the agreement was prejudiced against her and she was advised not to sign it. But Mr Kennedy said the wedding would be called off if she didn't. Ultimately, she signed, and they did get married.

After separating in 2011, Ms Thorne was living in Australia without a support system. The High Court found the figure she'd received in the divorce to be 'piteously small'. It also ruled that the binding financial agreement was 'entirely inappropriate and wholly inadequate'. Ultimately, the binding financial agreement was deemed unenforceable.

So it's important to note that when binding financial agreements are considered problematic, they can be 'set aside' at court because someone was under pressure or hadn't been given proper guidance. In other words, there's no point in drawing something up if you blatantly intend to pull the wool over your partner's eyes to protect your assets. It's important to consider that at the point of separation, both parties will be all right and able to support themselves.

According to Pepe, 'If one person would be at such an injustice because they put everything into the relationship and received no benefit when they exit the relationship, that binding financial agreement could be successfully challenged at court, and not be enforceable. You should aim to make sure the binding financial agreement contemplates the ups and downs of life.'

Indeed, uncertainty is the only real certainty we have in life, so the contents of an agreement made on the basis that 'two able-bodied people are able to earn income' is one thing, but if one member of the relationship falls ill or suffers an injury and isn't able to work, the agreement may also be challenged.

Binding financial agreements can be drawn up at any time in your relationship, not just when you're moving in together or getting married. 'It's best to do it when things are good between you. This way, you can plan and make decisions together when both of you are thinking clearly and sensibly,' Pepe says.

How much does a binding financial agreement cost?

Binding financial agreements are usually around $4,000–$10,000 (depending on the complexity), but some big firms can charge upwards of $20,000. Why so much? According to Pepe, in Australia, there are risks associated with binding financial agreements for both the parties and the lawyers which can include:

For the parties:

Lack of understanding: If the parties do not fully understand the agreement and its consequences, they may later regret their decision.

Unforeseen circumstances: The agreement may not take into account future changes in circumstances, such as the birth of a child or loss of income.

Unfair terms: If the agreement is not prepared and executed properly, it may be found to be unenforceable or unfair.

For the lawyers:

Liability: If the lawyer fails to properly advise the parties of the risks and consequences of the agreement, they may be liable for professional negligence.

Complexity: The law surrounding binding financial agreements can be complex and subject to change, which can increase the risk of making mistakes in preparation or execution of the agreement.

It is important for both parties and their lawyers to carefully consider these risks and ensure that all necessary steps are taken to minimise them. This includes the requirement of seeking legal advice preferably from experienced family law specialists and thoroughly reviewing and understanding the terms of the agreement before signing.

Protecting asset in a de facto relationship

In a de facto relationship where one person has a property in their name and the other moves into that property, it is wise to set financial boundaries early. If the non-owner party makes regular financial payments, you may agree that the money is a rental payment, rather than making room for uncertainty as to whether the payment is adding to the value of the property. A binding financial agreement can clearly set out and define the nature and intention of the payment (and any other payments or contributions made by either partner).

I took a sizable risk when Sam moved in, because he did add value to the house. Immediately. Six months into our relationship, he'd done an incredible amount of work, plastering, painting, replacing floorboards, installing new light fittings and more. Had we split up six months in, he'd have easily been entitled to make a claim on the house, not least because I was posting our renovation journey on social media so there was no shortage of proof.

I knew what I was doing. I knew there was a financial risk, and it was a risk I was willing to take. While we had an agreement, it certainly wasn't legally binding. And honestly, the reason why we didn't put our agreement in front of a lawyer is because it would have cost both of us a fortune. The reality is binding financial agreements are a huge expense for your average couple living in a country town, or anywhere for that matter. By no means am I saying that you should rule it out, but it can be highly prohibitive if you don't have large sums of money on hand. Importantly, if your de facto relationship does come to an end, you need to complete any financial settlement within two years. If you miss this timeframe, you need to apply to complete the settlement outside of the allocated window and the court decides whether this is approved or not. Often, it's only granted when you can show that you will experience hardship if it's not granted and there's a clear reason why it hasn't happened sooner. So, in this case, having a legally binding resource could be an excellent back-up.

Does a handwritten financial agreement ever hold up in court?

I've heard anecdotes from couples who 'wrote something down' in the form of typed up 'contracts' or even scribbles on pieces of paper. If funds are tight, can this ever be enough? According to family lawyer Laura Vickers, 'A handwritten agreement might be evidence of what one or more parties intended, which would be one of the factors a court considers in making a decision.'

So that's something, but the best chance of your agreement really sticking in court is if it's backed by legal advice. Laura says a self-drafted document just 'doesn't have the protections of the *Family Law Act* that requires a court to follow it, especially if it wasn't accompanied by both parties having the full picture of the other's assets and the benefit of independent legal advice for both parties'.

Research from the Australian Institute of Family Studies indicates that about '70 per cent of couples can resolve their end-of-relationship issues between themselves'. I find this heartening. I'd expected the number to be lower, and in fact assumed most people ended up in court. The AIFS reports that only about 3 per cent have to go to court, 6 per cent need lawyers to help them find a resolution and 10 per cent will use family dispute resolution.

Given binding financial agreements can come with a hefty price tag, it seems the expense could be difficult to justify if there is negligible difference between partners' assets at the beginning of a relationship. However, according to family lawyer Talya Faigenbaum, if there is a huge power imbalance that will likely emerge in court, the agreement could be overturned anyway. In which case stringent record keeping is your best bet for getting a fair outcome.

Couple goals check-in

No one likes to think about their relationship coming to an end, but if there are assets held by one of you, or both shared jointly, you need to talk about it. Here are some discussion points to consider:

- Have we adequately discussed what would happen to our assets if our relationship ended?
- If we run a business, what would happen to that business if we separated?
- Do we need a binding financial agreement?

CHAPTER EIGHT

Owning property together

All that chat about protecting yourself had me feeling pretty cynical. I know it's really important, but here's a wild question: What happens when people *do* live happily ever after?

I'm not for a second suggesting that people should bypass professional advice if they're coming to a relationship with an asset that they need to protect, but let's park the pessimism briefly and consider the fact that while almost half of marriages end in divorce, about half of marriages *don't* end in divorce. And, of course, this figure doesn't account for the many happy de facto relationships.

Despite this, most experts err on the side of caution when it comes to assets. I heard the words 'protect yourself' over and over. It made me feel like I should always have one foot out of my relationship, but that mentality can't be good for a couple. It seemed counter-intuitive to apply such individualistic advice across the board. Surely good healthy relationships can thrive financially when you commit to investing and building assets together?

One couple, two individual assets

It's not unusual for one or both members of a new relationship to already have their own assets and this can create issues when they begin making plans together. Among the challenges that come with having two individual assets in one relationship are the ongoing costs of maintaining them: two sets of council rates, two sets of strata fees if they're apartments, double the bills, plus the cost of any maintenance on both properties. There can also be emotional challenges: one partner might be reluctant to sell their property and they might try to hold onto it as a form of security.

According to Chris Bates, financial advisor turned property broker, there can be a lot of emotional attachment, particularly if the property has been home or they believe it's a good investment to hold. But the attachment may in turn prevent a couple from making the best decision for their future. He suggests, 'They need to ask what's best for them and commit to building wealth as a couple.'

Although it's important to get advice where required and have a plan in place for if the relationship ends, overall, if you're a committed couple, Chris believes, 'there should be a mindset shift to doing things together and an attempt to try to lose the emotional attachment to the original properties'.

Benefits of buying property together

It can help to consider the numbers and what it might look like if you did sell one or both of the original assets to purchase something else, always with your long-term lifestyle objectives in mind. You might find that together you can afford a 'forever home' rather than something smaller that won't suit you in a few years. Bates reckons a smart approach can be to think 'collectively rather than individually' to build wealth as a couple.

This strategy means you secure a higher quality asset, and bypass the costs associated with selling and buying all over again when you need to upgrade. You might realise that the place you can purchase together is much nicer and in a better location, which makes it a more attractive prospect in terms of both lifestyle and potential future value.

CASE STUDY

Sydney-based Anna, forty-four, and her partner Megan, thirty-six, were considering buying separately but committed to buying together to make a stronger financial move as a team.

Prior to building a relationship with Megan, Anna, who works in telecommunications, had intended to purchase her own property. This was after Anna's spouse of eight years took her own life in 2022. 'We had been saving up to buy our own place and were living with her parents to save money,' Anna says. In addition, Anna's partner had life insurance and some assets that Anna wasn't aware of.

With the savings and the additional funds that came from her partner's estate, Anna says, 'I was encouraged by her family and mine to look for my own place to live in and have forever.'

Now Anna is in a relationship with Megan, but initially, Anna was still looking to purchase a property solo. 'At the beginning it was always about me looking after myself and my financial future. At first I wanted to buy a small apartment outright with no mortgage and I didn't have many preferences or real emotion about it,' Anna says. She was thinking more about what she could get in her preferred location on Sydney's Northern Beaches, which is where her late spouse's family is from.

It was also an independent decision because Megan didn't have imminent plans to purchase. 'She had been saving as best she could, on nurse's wages, while paying rent in a sharehouse, so she didn't have enough for a deposit,' Anna says. At this point, they hadn't considered their shared borrowing capacity with two wages.

But that changed as Anna began to factor Megan into her plans as Megan is a specialist nurse and Anna didn't want her to have to commute long distances, particularly after late shifts. It was around this time that their broker advised her that 'it would be better long-term if I wait a bit before rushing into buying any old apartment. In the case this new relationship works out and we both decide to buy together,' Anna says.

Taking this approach meant that they could purchase a better property that would suit them for longer. 'Me buying an apartment now only wanting to sell in two years to get something family-sized would be a waste of money,' Anna points out. This would be due to the cost of stamp duty, buying and selling costs.

Anna admits some of her early decision-making was a result of feeling anxious about wanting a permanent roof over her head, but again their broker countered this argument. 'He said a big decision like buying a first property shouldn't be made based on just needing a roof over one's head.' Anna agreed with his logic and continued to rent with Megan until their plans for the future were firmer. Anna admits that this did help her to slow down and take a step back to see the full picture, not least because she had been grieving. 'I was half on auto-pilot and half-reactionary,' Anna says.

As time passed, and Anna found clarity, she began to discuss prospects with Megan in more detail. 'Originally the plan was going to be that she would just move in with me to my place, and just help pay the bills but not the mortgage and save for her own deposit on an investment property.'

This changed as they started inspecting homes together. They went to one that was out of Anna's price range, but Megan really loved it. Anna recalls, 'I think we would have needed another $200,000 to get a look in at that one.' With Megan's income improving their borrowing capacity, they realised it might actually be possible. So, Megan said to Anna, 'How about we do it together?'

The pair talked about it in detail and drew up a binding financial agreement to protect each other's contribution, but also to ensure they felt like equals. 'It was my place, but now it's our place,' Anna says.

Their shared borrowing capacity meant they were now looking at bigger places than Anna would have been able to buy on her own. It would also ideally be something that suited them for at least five years. Although it wouldn't be their 'forever' home. 'We would like to have a family one day and wouldn't be in this place long-term as we would like a house with a backyard. We planned to pay off this house as quickly as possible and look for the forever house.'

After beginning to make plans and seek pre-approval based on their incomes in November 2022, they were in a position to start making offers by February 2023. At that point, they were still taking their time because interest rates were rising and the supply of good properties was rising, too. 'We weren't afraid to walk away,' Anna says, standing strong on the decision to take as long as was required to find the right asset to share with Megan. Of course, improved borrowing power wasn't the only benefit of buying a property with a partner. 'Having a second brain is super useful. Megan has a different outlook and quite often she would point out something about a property that I hadn't thought about.'

Shortly after they secured their pre-approval, they bought a two-bedroom townhouse in the Sydney suburb of Wollstonecraft. After a short settlement, Megan and Anna moved in and started making it their own. Buying as a team meant they obtained a quality home with a large north-facing courtyard and beautiful timber floors. It's close to many amenities and gives them enough space to adopt a pet and start a family.

Ultimately, Anna says professional advice changed her whole approach to property ownership. 'My initial goal was not to become a homeless old lady, which is a very low bar. Now I understand borrowing power is an asset, as much as cash is.'

Anna and Megan believe that their decision to buy together, accompanied by the additional reassurance of a binding financial agreement, ensures they're both fully committed to a future that gives them a good safety net and a lifestyle that works for both of them. 'We don't want to be wealthy; we just want to be happy and safe,' Anna concludes.

Turning 'mine' into 'ours'

Anna and Megan provide a wonderful example of a couple who used their shared resources, but sometimes the imbalance is inevitable if one person had an asset to begin with. If the decision is to live in an asset that one member of the couple owned prior to the relationship, what are the rules for putting the other person 'on the mortgage'?

I'd always assumed that getting Sam's name onto the mortgage would be an important part in the process of turning my asset into ours, but there are lots of things for couples to consider here. At a functional level, it's easy enough to put a second person on the mortgage; after all it's just two people paying the loan.

But once a couple has done their due diligence and agreed this is an appropriate decision, they still need to consider the impact on their serviceability. Broker Chris Bates points out that the original owner needs to consider if they could still afford the loan in the event of a split. Timing is also important: 'If you go on parental leave or you become self-employed and there are servicing issues, you might not be able to do it,' he adds.

By contrast, does the second person have enough capacity for serviceability and a reliable credit rating to be added to the loan in the first place? For example, one partner might have a default on their credit card from an unpaid bill. The house might need to stay in the original owner's name.

The challenge with refinancing a property to add a partner's name is that you need to be in a suitable serviceability situation when you want to do this.

Here's another example: person one comes to the relationship with the asset, and person two is added to the mortgage. For a few years, life together is bliss. They go on to have a child and person one takes time out of the workforce or reduces their workload to a part-time capacity while they're focused on raising the child during preschool years. A tricky situation might arise if they were to break up. If neither one can afford to buy the other one out because they can't take on the mortgage solo, they'd have to sell the property. This could involve holding onto the property jointly for some time until the right opportunity to sell came along. In this case the couple would need to make a plan to move forward. It may mean continuing to work as a financial team after a separation for the shared financial benefit.

Selecting a quality asset

Clarifying your long-term goal can play a big part in your success if you intend to build wealth through property. Often people will only be thinking about the next five years, which can be limiting when they want to make their next move, especially when factoring in selling and buying costs such as stamp duty.

According to Chris, 'The problem with the upgrader stepping-stone strategy is the properties are growing faster,' meaning that by the time you're ready to buy something bigger, the prices in your ideal area may still be out of reach. This inevitably impacts the people who want to have families and need a bigger home than they would if it was just the two of them.

So daunting as it is, if children are on the cards, you are best served by thinking about this well in advance.

If you want to make money out of your property, Bates believes, the key is to choose a property that will always be in demand, but is of limited supply. For example, more high-density apartments can always be built. But on the flipside, there are only so many heritage family homes in established suburbs. These are gold-star assets because there will never be more homes like them. Bates also says there will always be demand for 'quiet streets, light and sun, good schools, communities and accessibility'.

Although it may feel counter-intuitive to ask yourself what kind of future buyer would want your home, this is a good way to test the quality of your asset and the potential for it to grow in value over time. Most importantly, it's crucial to ask yourselves, 'What sort of purchase is really going to help us achieve what we want as a couple long-term?'

Minimising property tax

There are many tax implications when it comes to property ownership and there's lots to consider depending on your personal circumstances. These days, with couples settling down at an older age than they once did, there's every chance that one or both parties will be reasonably financially established from the outset.

CASE STUDY

Jorja and Zac are thirty-five. When they met, they had both moved from Melbourne to regional Victoria. Jorja lived in a property that she was renovating, while Zac lived in a home half an hour away. Neither of them knew many people in their respective towns and used dating apps as a way to meet new people. Zac indicated in his dating profile that he was renovating his property, so they seemed to have plenty in common. Despite that, 'I had gone into the date ready for a break; our first date was meant to be my last for a while,' Jorja says.

But their shared passion for restoring properties helped them to build a bond quickly and see a future where their own personal goals could intertwine. 'The conversation grew to include each other in the plans,' Jorja says. This meant working out what to do with their respective properties to make a shared goal more impactful.

Part of the discussion regarding what to do when it came time to move in together was the tax associated with their individual assets. Prior to meeting, Jorja and Zac both lived in their principal place of residence. A 'principal place of residence' is a property that you own or have a mortgage on which is exempt from capital gains tax (CGT) because you live in it. By contrast, if you have an investment property, that property will be subject to CGT. A capital gain is the profit derived from an asset at the point you sell it. That gain becomes taxable income.

Here's a simple example.

You have a mortgage of $200,000 on a home, but you sell the home for $500,000 and you've made a profit of $300,000 (less agent commission and other sales costs). If you live in that home, that $300,000 is all yours. If it's an investment and you don't live in it, that $300,000 is added to your income and considered taxable. That said, there are several considerations regarding how much tax is payable, which we'll explore in more detail shortly.

As singles, Zac and Jorja would not have faced CGT if either of them sold their properties, but as their relationship progressed, they decided they wanted to move in together, which meant they had a few choices: Jorja could sell the home she lived in before moving in with Zac so that she could take any profit without CGT, or she could keep the property as an investment. As an investment, the property would qualify for CGT from the time Jorja moved out and a rental tenant moved in.

Zac could also sell his property or rent it out and move in with Jorja, facing the same implications. The third option was to sell both properties, pool their resources and buy something together.

'Originally Zac's intention for his property was for it to become an Airbnb,' Jorja says, explaining that they had family and friends test it out, but they decided there would not be enough reward for the work involved in running it.

Jorja also considered turning her home into an investment property, but at the time, she knew her fixed interest rate was ending in 2024, after which time it would run at a loss with rental tenants covering only some of the mortgage. Preferring not to subsidise the gap in income using her own cashflow and knowing that it had only ever been a stepping stone to something else, she decided to sell rather than drawing out equity to contribute to a new property with Zac.

Additionally, Jorja says the timing was right for several reasons. They had both finished their renovations. 'We both wanted a new project. Neither of us wanted to maintain an investment property and we also didn't want two mortgages to service at a time when interest rates were rising.'

Jorja and Zac decided to sell both of their properties and buy something new together in Daylesford so that they had one principal place of residence between them. Most importantly, though, the decision was aligned with their long-term goals. The property they purchased is still not their 'forever' home, as their plans are to keep renovating properties, adding value and building equity in the process. 'Ideally we hope to keep stepping up until we can afford acreage,' Jorja says.

It's no small undertaking, but their individual strengths – Zac's renovation skills and Jorja's experience in interior design and construction project management – make them an enviable team. 'Before meeting it was both our plans to renovate to add value to climb the property ladder and grow wealth. By coming together, we get to share our passion and plans. It was the natural decision for us,' she says.

For now, they are content in their current home, an 1880s cedar weatherboard cottage with a large extension at the back. 'It's liveable but has a lot of room for improvement,' Jorja says. 'The first thing you see from the front door is the main toilet,' she laments, so the floorplan will be rejigged to address this.

'Half the fun is watching this evolve as we get to know the property better,' Jorja says. There's lots to love in the meantime, including a huge Japanese maple and a small orchard that they're learning to care for. They will revive the garden that has been neglected for a few years and add a vegetable patch.

As Jorja points out, you can start with a strong long-term plan, but things can change over time. They are considering subdividing the bottom of the block and building a new house for themselves and turning the existing property into a rental. Although, she adds, 'We might fall in love with the block and not want to break it up. We don't need to subdivide to make a profit.'

They plan to be in the property for at least five years but are also realistic about their budget and the time it can take to get trades, particularly in regional Victoria. They're always considering the tax implications of their decisions, though. For example, if they were to subdivide the block, they would not be subject to CGT if they retain ownership of it. This would only happen if the block was sold. That said, if they did build on the back of the

> block and have a tenant in the front house, that property would be subject to tax associated with the rental income (effectively it would become an investment property that would be subject to CGT), so they may consider selling the front home after a subdivision, but they will reassess their position when the time comes.
>
> They've certainly thought of everything, and although they're rock-solid, they've still discussed the ramifications of a separation: 'Each of us would receive back what we put in, in terms of deposit, and then everything we make in equity would be split 50/50, although this would be reviewed if we ever have a child together,' Jorja concludes.

As mentioned above, when you own a property and you live in it, that asset is tax free as it's your primary residence.

If two people each own properties and they move in together into person A's property, person B's property is no longer their primary place of residence. As we've seen above, that has implications. So, if you're in that position, how do you decide which house to live in?

According to accountant Julian Mauro, 'It's not necessarily a decision based on whose property might be impacted by more of a capital gain; there are lifestyle choices. Timing is important too.' This is particularly true if you've lived in your property before it becomes an investment property. If you've held and lived in your property for five years and turn it into an investment for the sixth year when you move in with a partner, for five of those six years it was a tax-free asset and for one of six years it's taxable.

Julian says a simple way to estimate a capital gain is to understand 'what's the overall gain and how many years was it taxable'. Many people think that capital gains have their own tax rate but that's not the case. The total gain becomes part of your overall income, and you are taxed at the rate associated with the total income.

Capital gains are a section within your tax return where you're asked how much profit you made on the sale of an asset such as shares or property. In the case of a property, you add up all of the purchase costs including the cost of the property or mortgage, stamp duty, legal fees and then you compare that with sale proceeds including agent commission, advertising and additional legal fees. Whatever you're left with is either a gain or a loss. If it's a loss there's no capital gain.

According to Julian, capital gains are considered as part of your tax return in any given financial year and there can be many considerations if you're going to be in a position where capital gains are payable due to the sale of assets such as property.

An example might be where someone sells an investment property and makes a $100,000 gain after agent commission and sales costs. Julian says, 'If they've owned it for more than twelve months, the ATO gives you a capital gains discount and you pay tax on half of that which is $50,000. So, of that $100,000 profit, the seller needs to pay tax on $50,000.

That $50,000 is considered as part of your overall income in that financial year. Julian points out, 'If you have no other income, you pay the marginal tax rate of someone on $50,000. But if you have a salary of $200,000, and add the $50,000, you're getting taxed at the tax rate of someone on $250,000 which is a much higher rate.' (Salary of $200,000 plus taxable capital gain of $50,000.)

That total tax figure applies to the individual who held the property. But things change if you buy a property as a couple. We'll explore this in a moment.

Accessing the Bank of Mum and Dad

So far, I've assumed that if you're purchasing a home with your partner, you're doing it independent of family assistance. But it's worth noting here that the Bank of Mum and Dad, estimated to be worth about $35 billion in 2023, making it Australia's ninth-largest home loan lender, may also play a part in your path to home ownership. In other words, your folks or your in-laws might chip in to help you get into a property.

According to lawyer Laura Vickers, 'When parents have advanced funds, it is in everyone's interests to have it clearly documented whether this is a loan or a gift, and make sure the borrower child's bank is on the same page.'

This is where a binding financial agreement may really come in handy, because you need to be very clear on the loan terms. For example, if a family fight breaks out, can the parents call for the full amount to be repaid in thirty days?

Also your financial circumstances will still have implications for what kind of house you secure. 'Advancing funds via a loan agreement rather than a cash gift might mean the child cannot borrow as much as they need,' Laura says.

That's why it's essential to get legal advice before accepting financial input from your parents, as it can have several flow-on ramifications. These include:

Your bank: you need to make sure you're not misleading the bank in terms of whether the funds your parents put up need to be repaid or not

Centrelink: whether it breaches pension gifting rules

State Revenue Office: if the ownership structure impacts your eligibility for a stamp-duty concession

The ATO: if your parents are selling another property to provide the gift, they'll need to know what their capital gains tax obligations are.

The alternative is a guarantor arrangement which might be better because it can help to increase your borrowing capacity. But there are downsides to this approach, too.

Laura cautions, 'It does put the parents at risk though, as the bank can call on them to repay the bank loan if the children default, which could put their home at risk.'

Overall, what you need to know here is that if there is any family involvement, and things don't play out as planned, this doesn't just have financial implications, it could have a significant emotional impact, too.

Capital gains tax when you own property as a couple

Let's say you either don't own a property and therefore rent, or you own one property that is your principal place of residence and want to buy an investment property. If you buy together as joint tenants with a 50/50 ownership agreement, when you sell the property down the track, you'll need to declare 50 per cent of the gain each on your individual tax returns and this will be factored into your overall personal income tax. This means that one person might be paying more or less tax if one's on a higher income than the other.

Let's take that recent example, where the gain is $100,000 and you've held it for more than a year, so 50 per cent of the gain is taxable. It means you both have to add $25,000 to your total taxable income. Things get interesting if one of you made no income in the financial year, which means your total taxable income is just $25,000; if the other made $100,000 in salary, their total taxable income becomes $125,000 when the capital gain is added.

Once the property has been sold, it's not legal to declare that the ownership split was different. By this I mean you can't say, actually, the property was only in the name of the spouse who made no income this financial year and put the total $50,000 capital gain on their tax return.

That's why it's important to really think about the ownership structure prior to purchasing an investment property and look at the big picture in terms of costs for the duration that you intend to hold it. Capital gains aren't your only consideration, though.

Will the property be positively or negatively geared?

In other words, will the property make a profit or a loss each year? According to Julian Mauro, 'One of the biggest expenses is your mortgage repayments. When you look at your rental income minus your rental expenses, it's worth noting that only the interest portion of the loan repayments is a tax deduction, not the whole repayment itself.' So this is something to watch out for when establishing whether your property will make a profit or loss. On paper, the income made from your tenant might be less than your mortgage, but if you are on interest-only payments, for example, this is a deduction, so from a tax perspective you might end up making a profit.

Like capital gains, if the property is making a profit, that goes into your tax return as part of your total income.

'If your income is $200,000 and you made $10,000 through your rental income, you get taxed at a $210,000 tax rate.'

That means if you as a couple are in a similar situation with a property that's going to be generating a profit, you mightn't want it in the name of the person with the higher income, because they'll pay tax at a higher rate, but if it's costing you more than it generates in income – negatively geared – then you might put it in the name of the higher earner to reduce their tax rate.

'If it's making a profit, it makes less sense to put it in the name of the higher income earning individual, but if it's making a loss, it makes sense to go into the name of the higher income earning person,' Julian explains.

By contrast when you make a loss (if the cost of holding the property is more than the rent derived), that is treated as a tax deduction. 'If the cost of the property outweighs the rental income you make by $5,000, for example, you can claim a $5,000 tax deduction for the year,' he adds. In this case, it could make more sense to have the property in the name of the person who earns more, because they can reduce their taxable income this way. By contrast, if the property is going to be making a profit (i.e. generating income) you might then prefer to put the property in the name of the spouse who makes less.

But again, the way ownership is split will be a factor at the time you come to sell and you'll need to factor in the capital gains tax. So, if you decide to put the property in the name of the higher-income earner because it's making a loss that reduces their taxable income each year, does this logic go out the window if you later sell the property for a huge profit and they're hit with massive capital gains tax in their name only?

There's a stack of hypotheticals here, not least is the matter of income. You can never really be sure who's going to make more or less over time due to possible promotions, redundancy and time out of the workforce caring for children.

Setting up a property trust

The unpredictability of life can be one of the many reasons some people choose to purchase property in a family trust. While there are legal and accounting costs to set one up, there is more flexibility in terms of the way profits are split.

In a trust, every year you get to decide the percentages that get distributed to the family members in the trust. This can be beneficial as incomes ebb and flow. For example, when someone goes on parental leave and isn't generating income. According to Julian, you might decide to put the profits in that person's name because they will be taxed at a much lower rate than a partner who's working and generating a salary. Alternatively, you might split the tax on any profits 70/30, in line with relevant incomes in a financial year.

But again, it pays to think about how long you intend to hold a property (or properties) and whether the cost of setting up a trust is more effective than other structures.

'If you're going to buy a property and develop it into three units, it's going to be quite a profitable exercise,' Julian says and explains that in this case you might be wise to talk to your accountant and ask if a trust makes sense rather than putting a property in your individual names.

I'd always assumed that trusts were for people with heaps of money and a massive property portfolio, so I was surprised when I discovered the associated costs of establishing trusts, which are set up by accountants and solicitors. While the figures can vary, $1,500 to $2,000 is standard. This is not a huge outlay if the tax benefits stack up. You have a yearly tax return for the trust in addition to personal tax returns. This means you're looking at approximately $800 to $2,000 at the more complex end for additional tax return compliance work each financial year.

Overall the message is that the way you structure an investment will be unique to your situation and it can be hugely valuable to speak to an accountant or tax expert before proceeding so you don't end up paying too much tax.

Couple goals check-in

I know that property isn't something everyone is striving for, but for many couples it will be the biggest asset they share together. If that's you, have a chat about the following considerations:

- What are our long-term property goals, if any?
- If we brought individual assets to the relationship, how does this impact our financial position?
- Do we want to buy an investment property?
- If we had equity in our home, how would we use that money?
- If we purchase an investment property, how will we structure that investment from a tax perspective?
- If we have financial support from family, what are the implications if our relationship ends?
- Does a property trust make sense in our circumstances?

CHAPTER NINE

Should you put a ring on it? Marriage vs de facto relationships

On a quiet Thursday night in November 2022, Sam and I were having a glass of wine at home after work while listening to Phil Collins. During 'In the Air Tonight', I started banging on about my childhood, during which old mate Phil would frequently blast out of our huge 1980s stereo system that survived until my brother and I threw a house party in the early 2000s and blew the speakers.

At this point in my anecdote, Sam left the room. And while it was uncharacteristic for him to walk off on me while I was speaking, it's fair to say he'd listened patiently enough about the merits of Phil Collins during the six months we'd been together, so it was understandable that he'd reached his limit.

By the time 'Easy Lover' was playing, Sam had reappeared and was coaxing me to the kitchen to show me that he'd cleaned the coffee machine before I'd arrived home. I remember thinking, *I can't believe he's making me leave the comfort of the couch to see this.* I indulged him and had to admit that it was indeed very clean. When I turned around to thank him, he was down on one knee holding a ring box, asking me if I'd marry him. He told me he was asking here, in our home, because it is the most special place we spend our time, the physical foundations on which we're building a life together.

We'd talked about getting married. I personally don't think anyone should be surprised when they're asked to make such a significant decision and provide an answer on the spot, so this moment wasn't a complete shock. I'd given Sam a pretty clear idea of the kind of ring I'd like. We have a shared passion for pre-loved things: second-hand records, our perfectly imperfect old home. The ring was no exception: an incredible mid-century piece, crafted circa 1950. We often talk about the life it had before, who it might have belonged to and how it ended up in Ballarat where we found it.

I looked at a lot of rings. The one he chose was the one I loved the most and being vintage, it didn't come with an outrageous price tag. I didn't care how much he spent. I cared about the commitment that it represented.

He also told me that because we'd discussed the engagement, he wanted his proposal to be spontaneous, delivered in a moment that felt surprising to both of us, not at all contrived. And believe it or not, Phil Collins, our clean coffee machine and Sam's knee on our unpolished floorboards, carefully placed to avoid any rogue rusty nails, made it just that.

My answer was 'yes'.

We weren't in a rush to get married. I didn't get online and start researching dresses and venues, we just liked the idea of being engaged. And frankly, I struggled with the idea of parting with a huge wad of cash to pay for a wedding, not least because we were in the middle of a renovation.

Married vs de facto

In short, there's not much of a legal difference at all. If you get married, you might take your partner's name if that's something that's important to you. You also have to get a formal divorce if it doesn't work out. Because you're married and a divorce is required, any financial matters will be addressed accordingly.

By contrast, since 2009, people in eligible de facto relationships that have broken down can also apply to the court to have financial matters heard. To do this, you have to be able to say you were in a genuine de facto relationship and that you meet at least one of the following criteria:

- The period of your de facto relationship was at least two years
- There is a child or children from your relationship
- The relationship is or was registered under law in a given state or territory
- In the case of property and child custody, significant contributions were made by one party and failure to address this would result in a serious injustice.

In summary, if you have assets or children, there's very little difference between being married and being de facto where finances are concerned – there will inevitably be a financial separation either way. Though, as I mentioned in Chapter Seven, de facto couples must do this within two years. By contrast, according to the *Family Law Act*, married couples have twelve months from the date of a final divorce order to finalise their asset division.

We'll explore more of the implications of relationship breakdowns in an upcoming chapter, but right now let's assume you're happy and you want to make a commitment. The question is: What will it cost you and will that cost be worth it?

Financial advisor Jess Brady says that often couples overextend themselves during what should be the most exciting years of their partnership. 'There's a period of life that gets messy. Often people get married then turn their attention to property and having a baby. You're squashing three enormous financial events into a small timeframe.'

The compound impact of all of those experiences could result in serious financial ramifications. This means being realistic about where you are financially, particularly in the case of a wedding. As thrilling and wonderful as it can be, it's over in a heartbeat. With this in mind, it's worth working out what your long-term goals are and what you're willing to trade off before you get swept up and start handing over deposits to event suppliers.

Jess adds, 'With rising interest rates, you're putting an enormous amount of pressure on the general cost of maintaining a new beautiful life.'

According to the Bureau of Statistics, in 2021, more than 89,164 couples tied the knot, which is 21 per cent less than the 112,815 who married in 2019. The sharp decline can be attributed to the pandemic, but despite that, the number of couples formalising their relationship with a marriage has fallen since 2000, at which point the number of marriages per 1,000 residents was six, compared to 4.5 in 2019. Our peak of twelve per 1,000 residents was just after World War II.

There are many reasons for this, the first being an obvious redundancy of the traditional role of husband

and wife. Women are able to be financially independent without the need for marriage, society no longer expects children to be born in wedlock, de facto couples have the same rights and benefits of wedded counterparts. Oh, and it's really bloody expensive to have a wedding.

The wedding industry is a massive cash cow. Bridal stores in Australia are estimated to be worth $376.8 million. And that's just retail stores that meet bridal attire needs. Add the sectors that contribute food, drink, entertainment, make-up, photography and venues and it's astronomical. Not just for the couple, but often for the guests who attend pre-wedding events, often having to spring for accommodation and contribute to gifts, too.

It's easy to get sucked into, though. Sam and I initially planned to have a small engagement party in our backyard so we could introduce some of our family and friends who hadn't yet met. Everyone on our list said yes. Once we started looking into food and drinks, we knew we were already up for thousands. So, we began to wonder: *Should we just throw a ceremony in while we're at it?*

Sitting on our back deck one sunny Sunday, we looked at the cracked concrete path that would become the aisle, and the charming old shed that would be the backdrop to our altar, and agreed to throw a surprise wedding. It meant putting off the kitchen renovation a bit longer, but our pocket-money fund – the account we'd been putting small regular sums into – now had enough in it to cover a big chunk of the catering. Our aim was to stay under a total budget of $10,000.

We asked a friend to be our celebrant. This was really important because we wanted our ceremony to be fun, relaxed and meaningful. In our friend Beck, we had someone who knew our story. She was also an outstanding public speaker. The catch here was that she wasn't an actual celebrant. We arranged for a registered celebrant to do the legal marriage registry work for us the day before (this still came at a cost: official paperwork $750).

I thought I had a good grip on the situation – that I was the most chilled bride-to-be of all time throwing a wedding that even our guests didn't know was happening. But I did spend a couple of anxious days worrying about dresses. Given we'd decided to get hitched five weeks before our big day, having something made was off the cards, but I wanted to love my dress, I wanted to feel great. I knew the style I was going for, and it wasn't couture, it was a 60s style shift dress. The one I chose wasn't cheap at just over $1,000, but that was nothing compared to other gowns I saw priced anywhere between $3,000 and $8,000.

Any time I found myself pulled to something shiny that was out of the scope, I asked myself if it was going to have a positive impact on the experience for everyone. If it was mostly self-indulgent, I'd let it go. It wasn't always easy, though. I often slipped into the 'I'm only going to get married once' mindset. I spent about forty-eight hours fixated on what I considered to be the perfect pair of shoes. But the price tag was absurd. I asked myself if Sam or our friends and family were likely to have their day enhanced by what I was wearing on my feet. Ultimately, I was not Cinderella, and the answer was no.

I had to wonder, if people are spending thousands on an outfit, how much are they blowing on the whole event?

Well, according to research, the average Australian wedding costs about $36,000. The study shows that 82 per cent of couples access their savings, while 60 per cent take out loans and 18 per cent use credit cards to bankroll the celebration of their union.

Jess Brady says often couples don't decide what they can reasonably afford before they leap into planning their big day. 'Most people get very quickly swept up into wedding mania. Budgets get set, blown and recalibrated many times before the big day. Generally, the final budget is nothing like the original one,' she warns.

It was odd to be having this conversation at the same time that I was planning a last-minute wedding. In the past I would have said: *Honestly, it's just one day, stick to the budget.* But even I got caught up in the creeping justification: *We'll have the photos forever! I must get these decisions right!* Plus, our $10,000 budget was a number based on how much we had saved, and how much we wanted to have left afterwards, and we'd picked that number before we started making calls. It's difficult to establish a budget at the outset when you have no clue how much it's actually going to cost for the services of each vendor you engage. I was unaware that it could cost at least $2,000 for a small marquee, and more if they provide a dance floor. I guessed a DJ would be about $500 – they can cost thousands, too.

'Society has shoved unhelpful messages down our throat for years about needing the perfect wedding, house, holiday and lifestyle. For most Aussies the income you would need to actually live this "perfect" life is unrealistic,' Jess says. 'People don't care about the paper of your invitation, or if you got the plate and cutlery upgrade, or the intricate table details. They care about seeing you in love – and not stressed about money.'

But we can't place all of the blame on society. Human psychology has a lot to answer for. One study suggests that humans tend to place a higher value on the present, at the expense of their future, which often leads to overspending in the here and now. When the imminent future holds a wedding, you may find your present bias going into overdrive. The best way to stop your present bias from taking control is to be aware that it's there and be both critical in your thinking and intentional with your spending, knowing that significant financial decisions made now could penalise you in the future.

Unsurprisingly, Jess doesn't advocate going into debt to fund your wedding, saying you don't want to start your new married life paying off the debt of that one day.

By contrast, it's likely going to be better if you work as a team to compromise, communicate and tackle the financial challenges together. 'To wake up afterwards without a looming bill to pay means you both know how to have a plan and stick to it, so you can turn your attention to your next team goal and work together to achieve it.'

Also, almost one in two couples who stand at the altar and declare that their union will last forever are actually going to part ways with a divorce (and all the cost that comes with that) well before someone kicks the bucket.

I want everyone who chooses to get married to blissfully go the distance, but life is long and unpredictable, so I worry about folks going into debt to finance a celebration when they could use those funds to set up a happy life well beyond the wedding itself. I get that some people have families who contribute to the cost of their wedding, but let's say you fund the majority of it yourself. That sum of money, invested in the share market, for example, could help you to achieve some incredible couple goals.

I used a digital investment calculator to see what would happen if couples put the amount of money they spent on a wedding into shares and held them for ten, fifteen or twenty-five years, based on an average annual return of 8 per cent, which is what the ASX 200 has historically returned. These figures assume the initial investment is not added to over time. The figures rise dramatically if this initial amount is topped up regularly.

Wedding cost	Estimated total **10 years** later if invested in the ASX with an average return of 8 per cent	Estimated total **15 years** later if invested in the ASX with an average return of 8 per cent	Estimated total **25 years** later if invested in the ASX with an average return of 8 per cent
$30,000	$66,589	$99,208	$220,205
$40,000	$88,786	$132,277	$293,607
$50,000	$110,982	$165,346	$367,009
$60,000	$133,178	$198,415	$440,411
$70,000	$155,375	$231,485	$513,812
$80,000	$177,571	$264,554	$587,215

Obviously it's not my place to tell you how much to spend on a wedding, commitment ceremony or reception. I fully understand the appeal of throwing a beautiful event to celebrate your love. We did it, and the money we spent was invaluable in bringing our families together and making memories we'll never forget. But this table shows that the financial choices you make at the beginning of your life together could have significant positive or negative compounding impacts on the quality of your life together, depending on the priorities you have at this juncture.

The amount you spend on such a life event is entirely up to you, but it's worth considering what's important now without neglecting the future. What's your long-term vision and will a spending blowout now impact your chance of having it?

Commitment, your way

Many couples are not only re-evaluating the cost of a huge wedding, plenty are turning to alternative experiences that come without an exorbitant price tag. It's not exactly shocking that young couples are taking issue with the expense of traditional weddings. If you're trying to save a house deposit, pay down student debt or, you know, buy groceries, you're probably not all that keen on shouting dinner and drinks for 100 of your nearest and dearest.

There are other personal benefits, too. An intimate event can be really true to you and your relationship. Marrying age is also a factor. It's not unusual for people to wait until their late thirties and forties to make a commitment for the first time, sometimes after they've had their kids. Then there are the many second marriages to consider.

According to marriage celebrant Kahani Motiani, 'With more and more couples choosing to have children before marriage, we've also seen that this is definitely impacting some couples' priorities and is reflected in the way they choose to wed. What these couples expect from the day (compared to what they say they *would* have wanted pre-kids) is sometimes poles apart.'

How to avoid going over budget

In her experience, Kahani says going over budget is 'absolutely the norm' for most couples because they often lock in a wedding date and a venue for fear of missing out.

That often means picking a popular time of year (spring, for example) in a picturesque (and costly) location, without a full understanding of the cost of the suppliers, 'or what sort of peak costs come with their chosen date'.

Peak wedding season can be a drain on finances. Want a Saturday in late spring or early autumn? Caterers, musicians, photographers and florists will charge a premium for that.

Kahani adds: 'Putting all the expectation on that one very expensive, stress-fuelled day to be "utterly perfect" and "the best day of your life" can seem – even to us in the industry – a little ridiculous. You get the best bang for buck if it's a true *experience.* One that was genuinely fun, preferably.'

Here are some expert tips for great weddings that don't blow the budget:

- Try an off-peak wedding day, such as Thursday.
- Consider a micro-wedding, which can be similar to a traditional wedding, but with guest numbers of no more than about thirty.
- Could you elope? With only a handful of guests or just your witnesses, the focus is squarely on you.
- Give the engagement party a miss (or follow the path Sam and I took, adding a surprise ceremony to the party).
- Do some research before you lock in a budget.

- Agree on your top three non-negotiable spends, put your money towards those and sacrifice elsewhere.
- Keep track of what you're spending as you go.
- Avoid getting sucked into the details no one will notice or recall after the event. Ask yourself if the guests' experience will really be enhanced or whether you could let it go.

Backyard wedded bliss

At 3pm in March 2023, our friends and family started trickling in for our engagement party. I had hired a dress for that portion of the event given I was only going to be wearing it for a few hours. Just before 6pm, we flipped the switch. Sam and I disappeared with our 'team' while a couple of our great mates who were in on it, Matt, Margot and Adam, went to work, setting up an aisle, positioning the arbour we'd hidden behind the shed and handing out paper cones filled with flower petals. When some of our guests realised what was happening, they got on board and helped too.

On schedule, Sam burst through our back door and into the garden in white jeans, a white shirt and a rich rose-coloured velvet jacket. He danced down the aisle with his uncle James, his dad Dan, and our dog Frankie. He handed out roses and met our friend Beck at the altar to wait for me.

Next, my ringbearer Nick and flower girls Arya and Cleo made their way down the aisle followed by me, along with my dad. The ceremony was intimate, funny and true to us. Our vows were personal. Afterwards, we had a few quick photos together, held speeches, had a first dance and partied with our mates.

Our surprise backyard wedding was definitely the experience we'd hoped for. Carefully planning the key musical moments, plotting the transition between engagement party and wedding and curating the theatre of it all kept our adrenaline pumping. We aimed for plenty of authenticity, humour, heart and tried to ensure that our biggest expenditure was on things that would give the people we love a joyful experience.

Did we stay within our $10,000 budget? No, we didn't. In the end we spent almost $13,000, and that included everything from our outfits and rings to decorations, photography, food and drinks. The biggest mistake was hiring a marquee that was far too big for the space, having it removed before the event and losing our $1,500 deposit in the process. We had to find a replacement dance floor forty-eight hours out. Planning a wedding during a time of high inflation also hit us. Everything was more expensive than we'd expected it to be, but there were areas that we saved.

We didn't have a full wedding photography package; our photographer was only there for a few hours. The flowers weren't part of a bridal package; for my bouquet, a local florist sourced peach dahlias from a nearby flower farm and wrapped some ribbon around them. Some of our spending went into last-minute home improvements, which benefited us in the long-term. The catering was an affordable carvery. Our wedding rings, like my engagement ring, are vintage. There was no cake. We borrowed chairs and styled the garden with stuff we already had.

Most importantly, the venue was our home, which meant everything to us. We achieved our goal: shock, delight and a day full of love, without going into debt. We'd also done a loose projection and knew we'd be able to top up a large chunk of the savings we used within about six months.

Would I do it again knowing how much it was actually going to cost? Absolutely. Because we value our friends and family and loved putting on a show for them. But I wouldn't have wanted to spend any more than we did, because it would have reduced our capacity to take on other projects we had planned in the near future. That said, I recognise that we were able to do this at a cost much lower than the Australian average because there was no family expectation of a huge traditional event.

Couple goals check-in

Weddings are extraordinarily fun, but they're also a lot of work and can be stressful to organise, especially if you're not financially set up to throw the event you'd like. Make sure you ask yourself these questions and also consider any big costs that you anticipate after your special day. Ideally you won't have a financial hangover after you get hitched.

- If we plan to have a wedding, are all of the aspects of the day aligned with our values?
- Will our wedding spending restrict our ability to do other things in the year that follows?
- Are we staying true to ourselves without hindering our long-term financial goals?
- Would we consider eloping or holding a micro-wedding?
- Is our budget realistic?

CHAPTER TEN

Small humans, big bucks

What comes after marriage? For many couples, it's starting a family, which, for the fortunate ones, is a relatively pleasant process. But for others, the path to parenthood can cause enormous relationship strain and heartache. In 2020, one in eighteen of the 295,976 children born in Australia were conceived with IVF – almost 17,000 babies total. In that year, more than 87,000 people completed a cycle. The quest to become a family can really add up if medical intervention is required.

CASE STUDY

A blind date in 2012 set Melbourne-based Aimee on a path towards a long-term goal that would take the best part of a decade to achieve. On that date, she met the man who would become her husband. Early in their relationship, they established that they wanted to have a family together but were already aware of their individual reproductive challenges. If they wanted to make their dream a reality, it was going to take everything they had, both emotionally and financially.

'I have always been very organised with budgeting and saving,' says Aimee, thirty-seven. Today, the pair have savings funds for several areas of their life including holidays, children's education, health, home maintenance, cars and fun times. Each time they're paid, the couple allocates income for each account.

They married in 2017, five years into their relationship, but at this point, they were already in the depths of their medical journey to have a child. Knowing early that infertility was a shared battle, Aimee and her husband began putting $200 a fortnight into an IVF account and adding any additional spare income such as bonuses.

'It was non-negotiable; we were having children,' Aimee says, but they didn't want this to be at the cost of their financial health, so their eyes were always on their IVF account balance to ensure they could cover any cost that they were presented with upfront and in full.

This is an extraordinary feat when you consider the fact that an egg collection will leave the average couple about $5,000 out of pocket, while an embryo transfer will be about $2,300 after rebates. They also had private health insurance and a family Medicare card, which meant their combined medical costs got them to the maximum rebate safety net threshold fast (in 2023 it's $2,414, a threshold that is achieved with one IVF cycle).

But that's just the beginning. 'If you are lucky enough to have viable embryos after an egg collection, you can have genetic testing and that's $500 an embryo,' Aimee says. In some cycles, when they were lucky to get four embryos, that was an extra $2,000. That's an optional expense, but 'if you don't test them and choose just to transfer, you run the risk of miscarrying or them not implanting and later finding out they were abnormal; you've wasted your time and money'.

These are just the big expenses. Add specialist appointments, medication, storage fees and the natural therapies they both used, including acupuncture and naturopathy – it's an extraordinary investment. Aimee and her husband were just one of tens of thousands of couples doing the same thing.

Money aside, what kind of toll does this take on a relationship? Aimee says they were 'lucky' because they both had infertility problems. 'We didn't feel pressure from one another because we both experienced it, which is unique. We were equal in it.'

Aimee has seen the process break other couples, but says she's grateful that 'it wasn't all on me as the woman'. Over the course of seven years, they completed fourteen cycles, not of all these even ended with a viable embryo to transfer. Their daughter, Lucy, now four, was conceived on their fourth attempt, and their son, Toby, arrived on their final cycle.

In that time, Aimee went through egg collection five times, costing the family a total of $25,000. Then there was the $11,000 worth of embryo transfers, $4,000 in genetic testing, seven years of specialist appointments, medication and natural therapies. All up, Aimee estimates they spent somewhere in the vicinity of $63,000. But this was not something that caused conflict because they were always saving and preparing for their costs in advance. 'We had a lot of things that caused us pain, but money wasn't one of those things,' she says.

It was an all-encompassing goal that fortunately resulted in their two healthy children. But sometimes the challenge that comes with having a vision that takes so long to realise is working out what to do once you've made it.

Initially, Aimee simply looked forward to getting herself back. She was still breastfeeding Toby in 2023, but for the most part it was the first year in seven years that her body was hers again. 'During IVF, you can't just take a week off and go away because your body is need for procedures,' Aimee points out.

So for now, their new shared goal is to enjoy the fruits of a seven-year labour of love: life as a family.

The cost of parental leave

Kids are undeniably expensive, but having one, or both, of you stepping out of the workforce for an extended period of parental leave could cost a whole lot more.

In October 2022, as part of the federal budget, the Albanese government released a dedicated 'women's budget statement'. The 85-page national strategy document highlights the fact that in 2022, Australia sat in position 43 out of 146 countries assessed in the World Economic Forum Global Gender Gap Index. The paper outlines plans for more affordable childcare, expanded Paid Parental Leave benefits, changes to workplace relations laws to close the gender pay gap, and more funding to stop violence against women.

This is positive stuff, but I'd argue that government funding can only take us so far.

The strategy 'outlines a range of initiatives aimed at "moving the dial" through an overarching commitment to advance gender equality, under which there is a focus on four key themes: women's economic equality, ending violence against women, leadership and decision-making, and women's health and wellbeing'.

Great, but where are the blokes in all of this? Where's the bit about male partners taking on more domestic labour so that women can return to work in a way that's actually feasible? Why isn't there anything about a division of superannuation when one partner is staying home in a child-rearing capacity? Why aren't we having a discussion about couples managing their finances and career aspirations equitably during parenting years so that one person isn't significantly worse off in terms of skills, career progression and superannuation?

There's still a huge societal shift in thinking required. In a typical heterosexual relationship, a new father will continue to work, grow their experience and income (and therefore continue to build superannuation), while women are primarily stepping out of the paid workforce for the duration of their parental leave, sometimes longer, and occasionally, permanently.

Federal treasury research indicates that having children results in a dramatic gender-based income gap. 'Women's earnings are reduced by an average of 55 per cent in the first five years of parenthood,' the research says. It deems this a 'motherhood penalty' which is considerable, a full decade into parenthood. And women experience the penalty, even when they're the higher earner in the relationship. The penalty is not just financial, career satisfaction drops off too, beginning about a year prior to having kids. Why a year earlier? Well, talk to anyone who is employed and actively trying to conceive, they're probably not shopping around for a new gig. Once pregnant, all manner of factors discourage a woman from seeking a new job, including a need to receive parental leave benefits, anxiety associated with job interviews while pregnant, illness, commutes and more.

It's a vicious cycle with the research also indicating that after they have children, 'mothers experience a decrease in satisfaction with their employment opportunities, in line with their worsening employment outcomes'.

Additionally, two indexes illustrated in the research show that fathers are more likely than mothers to report that their work affects their family life, while mothers are more likely than fathers to say that family life affects their work. Put simply: it's hard for women to raise children when they're the primary carer and keep up a career, too. No surprises there.

These are among the challenges we face in a system that still largely assumes that a woman will be the primary carer, although some small progress is being made. Prior to 2023, Australians were eligible for eighteen weeks of Parental Leave Pay for a primary carer and two weeks of Dad and Partner Pay.

From 1 July 2023, Parental Leave Pay and Dad and Partner Pay were combined into one twenty-week payment, with the introduction of gender-neutral claiming that allows either parent to take that time. The family income limit to take paid parental leave is now $350,000, up from the previous individual income limit of $156,647. Parents can also take their leave in blocks as short as one day at a time over the course of two years from the child's birth or adoption.

Starting from 1 July 2024, Parental Leave Pay will increase by two weeks each year. This is until 1 July 2026 when it will reach twenty-six weeks. Your employer is obliged to pay this if you've worked for the company for at least a year before the birth or adoption of a child. If you're self-employed, the government provides the payments.

It's a baby step when you compare it with other OECD nations, though. Take Finland, where each parent gets 160 paid days of leave. That means the total leave available when split between both parents is more than fourteen months. Latvia offers ninety-four weeks, Japan fifty-eight and Poland fifty-two. The average as of late 2022 was 50.8.

Back in Australia, it's clear that even with the nudge to twenty-six weeks, the parental leave equation doesn't work here. We have some of the highest property prices in the world, so those child-raising years are inevitably harder when couples are shouldering massive financial burdens in the form of mortgages, rents and student debt. Parental Leave Pay is currently $882.75 per week and doesn't include superannuation. Parents return to work only to begin forking out for childcare. It's remarkable that large numbers of people in their child-raising years aren't moving to countries that provide conditions in which young families can thrive rather than scramble to make it work.

But, I digress …

Baby super

Once you've used your twenty weeks (or twenty-six weeks by 2026), you either have to return to work or continue in an unpaid leave capacity, so it's essential to work with your co-parent. Chances are the bare minimum paid leave won't be enough to supplement your traditional earnings.

Aside from that $882.75 being a pretty modest sum when one half of a couple steps out of the workforce to care for a newborn, the real kicker is the lack of superannuation. A recent survey by the Association of Superannuation Funds of Australia (ASFA) shows that women retire with an average superannuation balance of 23 per cent less than men. This shows that women taking time out to have kids absolutely cop it when it comes to superannuation generating capacity. Although, the findings also indicated, unsurprisingly, that this gap could be closed if superannuation was paid during periods of parental leave.

It's not just the missed super contributions of their male counterparts at the time; it's the massive compounding growth that's lost over decades. So, if you are intending to be, or have been a primary carer for children, is it fair for your working partner to end up with significantly more in super when the two of you retire? Perhaps it's okay if you're still together and you intend to share it. But what happens if you split?

If having children is a mutually agreed decision and raising small people is a hell of a lot of work, shouldn't both of you be adequately compensated during this time? You mightn't be able to rely on the government or your employers to create the equality you deserve, but as a couple, you have more power than you may realise.

'Financial planning associated with children should be a regular topic of conversation ideally before you even consider trying to conceive,' says Jess Brady. In her experience, 'Women believe they have to self-fund their parental leave, even if they're in a relationship.'

In some cases, this might be because women have been working for decades and aren't used to being dependent on their partner financially but there is an option to approach it as a team and share the burden.

Financial planner Rebecca Pritchard often sees couples who have historically worked well on their shared financial future revert to an individualistic mindset. 'It's sadly common to hear the breakdown of "us" into "me" and "you" during periods of parental leave.'

'Systemically, it's reinforced repeatedly,' Rebecca notes and says she has experienced this first hand. She started working when she was fourteen. The first home she bought with her husband was purchased predominantly with money she had saved. But when she went on parental leave, the documents told her that she was no longer the strong independent woman she'd always been. 'On forms I was listed as a dependent, because I wasn't working in that moment. It was infuriating and demoralising,' she says.

Rebecca says the parental leave structure creates a drastic imbalance. The penalty when someone carries, births and cares for a child in those early months and years is both financial and emotional. Even if you've always had an equitable relationship, you'll likely need to work much harder to maintain it when parental leave is taken. The key is to recognise there's a financial penalty for the primary carer, but you don't need to wait for the fiscal policy to catch up, you have other options.

CASE STUDY

Jacqui is a Yorta Yorta woman working as a mental health social worker, doula and yoga teacher. She'd known her partner for about fifteen years before they started dating when she was thirty-one. Jacqui bought her first property in 2021. Although she was in a relationship, it's only in Jacqui's name. 'It's in my name because it was my grandmother's home and it was my dream to have it, not his,' she says.

Jacqui is now thirty-six and the couple had their first child in September 2022. Until that point, they split all expenses equally and her partner paid 'rent' that was a bit less than half of the mortgage.

'I have a tendency to overpay for things and over support others so boundary-wise it was important for me to keep it all really clear,' Jacqui says.

The couple was planning to get married in 2022 prior to Jacqui falling pregnant, so they put that plan on hold, but when the time comes, her partner will pay for the wedding because it's something he wants, while Jacqui doesn't mind either way.

He is a qualified plasterer, and had two cars prior to their relationship. Jacqui also had two cars – one for work and a ute for work on the property – so her partner sold his cars, paid out his debts and started saving. Although they have had largely separate finances, they are working towards a shared goal. He purchased a log splitter and trailer and plastered the house, while Jacqui paid for additional renovations.

'The longer-term plan is to subdivide (it's a large block) and he will get the loan for the building of our dream home on that block,' Jacqui says. The property they're currently in will become holiday or family accommodation, then they will move into the larger home.

But, while Jacqui was on parental leave, her partner covered the mortgage until Jacqui went back to work. Prior to the arrival of their baby, they'd discuss what would happen if they split up. 'He would take one of the cars which I own outright and $10,000.

This seemed fair given he was debt-free, and I have paid for the home and the renovations for us to live comfortably.'

But the longer they're together, the lines of any future division of assets become blurred. 'At this stage, legally he is entitled to a share of the home given we live de facto but it's something we need to iron out.'

Jacqui's childhood experiences with money inform many of her decisions. Prior to parental leave, she had $30,000 saved to protect herself if anything went wrong. 'This was a tricky transition for me to depend on someone else,' she says. Jacqui hasn't given her partner key banking details. By contrast, he has shared his banking information with Jacqui and trusts her to spend money as needed. 'I don't know if I would give out my banking information to anyone. That's my issue though because my parent was really bad with money due to gambling, and I learnt as a child that it wasn't safe to have savings a partner or husband could access.'

While they're planning a happy future together, Jacqui shows her love and appreciation through her own approach to generosity and trust. 'Because I would typically earn more than him, I buy a lot for the home and for him. Not because he asks me to or expects it but because I like nice stuff and love giving gifts.'

> It's a delicate balance for Jacqui and she's realistic enough to know that relationships can change, so she's invested in their vision, but also regularly considers their individual finances. 'I think you can have the most amicable fair plan but in the end some separations go badly. I just hope that wouldn't be the case for us.'

Jacqui was lucky to be in a situation that allowed her to save plenty of emergency funds prior to parental leave, but I know not everyone has this option. So, how can you better manage your superannuation when one person is taking extended leave?

Here are some options:

Concessional contributions

Concessional contributions are any sums paid into your super account that receive a lower tax rate. These contributions are taxed at 15 per cent (if your income and contributions total less than $250,000) – for many Australians, this will be lower than the rate they pay on their taxable income. If you or your partner make these contributions any time in a given financial year, the person who makes the contribution can claim the deduction in their tax return. The concessional contribution cap is $27,500.

According to accountant Julian Mauro, there can be further tax benefits if you're earning less than $37,000 a year. 'Your spouse can contribute up to $3,000 into your fund and they can claim an 18 per cent, $540 tax benefit.'

But Rebecca points out, 'very few people do that because it's coming at a time when your expenses are at their highest and income is at its lowest'.

Splitting super

Splitting your super enables the working partner to transfer a portion of their contributions into super that year from their account to yours. To do this, you must be legally married, in a relationship that is registered under relevant state or territory laws or live together in a de facto relationship.

This is an equitable path to take, because there are no additional out-of-pocket funds required, but the superannuation that does come in is distributed across both members of the couple. This approach helps the working partner feel like they're reducing the financial hit to the person who takes the lead on childcare and also shows the value the carer makes to the family.

This can be done at any time, not just when someone is on parental leave, no matter how old your kids are. Similarly, it doesn't only apply to periods of child-rearing. It can be done at any time that one partner takes time out of the workforce to study or explore other opportunities. I could transfer some of my super to Sam if he were to take a few months off to renovate the house.

There's great potential in this option for many couples, not just those who have kids.

Rebecca also points out that it doesn't have to be a tidy 50/50 split. For example, let's say a woman had 50 per cent of her normal super contributions at that time, her partner could contribute 25 per cent of his to her fund. As a couple, they could take his total down to 75 per cent and her up to 75 per cent.

Then if the woman goes back to work part-time and has 60 per cent of her regular super coming in, the couple could then split their super so they both achieve 80 per cent. Whatever you decide to do in your circumstances, it's simple enough to sign the form and start the process. This solution allows you to take appropriate steps in your circumstances to retain superannuation equality.

Family friendly employers

The alternative to hustling to better manage your super as a couple during your kids' early years is to have a job with a progressive company. The bad news is there aren't a lot of them around. The good news is the number of companies providing more than the minimum is growing.

Some leading companies now pay superannuation while their employees are on parental leave and some are waiving the waiting periods. Traditionally, in most cases, employees would need to be working at a company for at least twelve months up to the date of their child's birth to access benefits, but progressive companies are offering entitlements from their employees' start date in order to attract and retain talent. On a practical level, this means people who are pregnant at the time they're hired are eligible to receive the company's parental leave benefits.

Those with best practice offerings include consulting firms KPMG and PwC, both of which offer twenty-six weeks of paid parental leave for parents, plus twelve months of super on both the paid and unpaid parental leave that is taken. Both organisations provide the option to take the leave in a solid chunk or split it across several periods of time up to the child's second birthday. Over at Energy Australia, new parents who return to work part-time will continue to be paid superannuation at their full-time rate until their child is five.

If you're lucky enough to work at Spotify, you get six months of paid parental leave no matter how you become a parent. Whether people use donor-assisted reproduction processes or choose to adopt, they're all treated equally when it comes to taking parental leave. On top of that, Spotify introduced additional family benefits in 2021 giving every employee across the global team a lifetime allowance for IVF, donor services and egg freezing and adoption. An extraordinary part of the employment package when both IVF and adoption can cost future parents tens of thousands.

First-baby economy

Of course, given how few Australian companies are offering parental leave packages that go above and beyond the bare minimum, many parents-to-be have no choice but to save their hearts out in the lead up to welcoming a child.

It's not just saving for children that's a consideration, but your spending habits too. Along with all the anticipation of the first child comes the risk of getting caught up in the 'first-baby economy', Jess Brady cautions. Prospective parents are hit with a barrage of marketing messages and cultural expectations and this begins well before the baby arrives, resulting in parents fearing judgement if they don't have certain things.

As with weddings, taking a step back can help you to escape the expectation spiral. Ask yourself what's essential, and what would be nice to have. The money you *don't* spend in the lead up to bub's arrival could go towards making life easier in those early years and contribute towards a family holiday or housing costs. The desire to have an Instagram-able nursery can be a trap, too. I don't remember the rooms I slept in before the age of three. And although I see the appeal of sweet rooms with coloured walls and decal art, designer cradles, bookshelves and bunting, they're not essential in your early days caring for a newborn.

What's often lost in the conversation when it comes to babies is the expenses required for mothers such as maternity clothes, vitamins, women's health appointments, new bras and other necessities. The partner who's not growing the human might be surprised by some of the expenses. 'It's not that they don't want you to buy a new bra because your boobs don't fit in the old bra; it's just that it never crossed their mind,' Rebecca says.

Pre-baby purchases

The challenge is that many couples just aren't financially prepared for a new baby. By the time you find out you're expecting a baby, you're already a month or so in. You don't work up until the day the baby comes so that only leaves six or seven months. That's not long to get organised.

According to research, during pregnancy things such as hospital bags, baby clothes and products, maternity clothes and food can cost $5,522; while one study found it can be more than $9,000 if you go beyond the basic set-up. These figures don't account for private healthcare, which can be in excess of $5,000 out of pocket. Ultimately, you can't budget for your child until you've made decisions about your priorities. The key is to have a clear understanding of all of the things that are essential, the items you *might* need and what's nice to have.

CASE STUDY

Patti and her partner, Joseph, were living in Sydney and trying to save a house deposit when they found out Patti was pregnant. 'It was a massive shock,' Patti says, and it took Joseph about two weeks to come to terms with it. So, it goes without saying, they weren't preparing financially for a child. They had a bit of a budget, but Patti also spoke to a lot of friends who gave her a sense of what they'd spent. She also did additional research.

It wasn't until she was pregnant that Patti realised parents-to-be were often totally clueless about the impending financial impact until a due date was looming. 'How does everything cost so bloody much?' Patti and Joseph asked themselves frequently in the lead up to their daughter Zali's birth in January 2020. To reduce their costs, they searched digital marketplaces for second-hand finds. Joseph, a carpenter, was able to restore great nursery furniture, such as their cot. 'We weren't precious about having seconds and thirds,' Patti says.

The couple were renting and had jobs, but they were also trying to save a house deposit, which is no easy feat in Sydney, where they were living at the time and paying $605 per week in rent. For Patti and Joseph, finding a way to secure a permanent home was now essential to them.

Patti and Joseph were happy to pay the medical costs associated with having Zali but because the pregnancy wasn't planned, they didn't have private health cover for obstetrics, which generally has a

> twelve-month waiting period (that's twelve months from admission to hospital for birth, so a few months prior to conception). Patti had Zali at Royal Women's Hospital and she says she was grateful to live near to such a good public hospital, where she had an emergency caesarean. They had been saving for out-of-pocket costs but, with the exception of some specific nutritional costs, antenatal classes and minor medical expenses, bringing Zali into the world cost them very little.

The cost of parental leave

The amount you'll need during any periods of parental leave will depend on whether or not the household income is going to be reduced, and what the impact is on your current budget.

So, for example, if you're a dual income household, how much income will you lose, and for how long? The amount you might want to save will have to cover all the expenses that occur during the period of unpaid work.

Let's say, hypothetically, that the person who is taking parental leave contributes $2,000 to your monthly household cost of living and they'll spend the first six months at home raising your newborn. That's $12,000 that you'll likely want on hand (of course, you may alter this figure depending on the parental leave benefits that you're entitled to).

According to Jess Brady, 'You need that amount in cash. Ideally, you would also have knocked off bad debt and have a healthy savings buffer of a few months of expenses up your sleeve should anything unexpected arise.'

What if you're not financially ready?

Jess knows that not every pregnancy is planned – surprise pregnancies aren't a new phenomenon. But the cost of living was comparatively much lower for generations past, and there's no doubt that the financial impact of having a family, especially if you're not ready, can be immense. In this case, Jess says you need to implement a strict budget and check out your parental leave entitlements to understand whether you qualify for government support.

CASE STUDY

Patti says in her experience navigating parental leave payments had plenty of challenges. Joseph, who is from the UK, was on a skilled migrant visa at the time. 'He couldn't get parental leave benefits,' Patti says. Patti is a Papua New Guinea-born Australian citizen who was entitled to government paid parental leave, along with benefits from her employer, but her big watch-out for parents-to-be is to lodge all of the paperwork associated with paid parental leave before the baby arrives if you're relying on it. Patti says that she knew several parents who were waiting on the payments after their child was

> born because they didn't submit the documents on time or their baby arrived earlier than expected.

Importantly, Jess adds that it's not the time to bury your head in the sand if you have debt. You can call your bank and potentially get financial hardship arrangements. Don't be afraid to call the national debt helpline. You may also find ways to bring in more income ahead of your baby's arrival. Remember that your love for your baby has nothing to do with whether they have a top-of-the-line pram or a wardrobe of expensive clothes.

Finally, while we live in a far more individualistic society than we once did, there's no shame in telling friends and family when you need support. This is not just financial, but emotional too. You need a team that's on board to support you as a couple in those early months.

Childcare

Of course, the first few months with a baby are only the beginning, and the complexity of managing money as a family will grow and change if both of you intend to return to the workforce.

Jess argues, 'We do not do enough forecasting and modelling about childcare,' and suggests that it's imperative to discuss the cost of care regularly and well before paid support is required. This can be harder to prepare for, because in the sleep-deprived haze of those early months and years, you mightn't have any idea what a future return to life with two incomes may look like.

CASE STUDY

Patti and Joseph know all too well that the cost of childcare can have a huge impact on other goals. Zali's first year of childcare cost the couple a staggering $26,000. With rent of $605 per week, they spent $60,000 on childcare and housing alone, but they sucked it up for a few reasons. First, Patti was in a contract role that wasn't ending until late 2021. Second, they were in the depths of Covid lockdowns, and couldn't have moved to somewhere more affordable even if they'd wanted to.

When they started searching for suitable childcare centres, they weren't sure if they would be entitled to rebates and some centres in their local area charged more than $200 per day. In the end, they were eligible for rebates, and they chose a centre that cost them $520 per week after subsidies.

They started transitioning Zali into childcare at eleven months, and Patti recalls having 'massive mum guilt'. She regularly wondered why she was working to pay for daycare fees, only to have two out of seven days a week with her daughter. 'If I could stay at home then I would have, but because of my contract I had to go back to work,' she says.

The upside is they were still able to save because they were locked down. During that time, they began plotting a move to Queensland, where they could afford to buy a family home and significantly reduce their childcare costs. Though Patti points out that childcare is never just about the money alone. 'We were paying a lot but the service and care provided by the educators is fantastic. They are worth their weight in gold.'

Patti's experience has led to her becoming an advocate at The Parenthood, a not-for-profit that advocates for adequate paid parental leave, family friendly workplaces and universal access to high quality early childhood education. Today, Patti and Joseph are happy in the Queensland home that they're slowly renovating together. They've reduced their childcare costs to $300 per week, and the savings helped them to offset mortgage increases as interest rates rose. It's a great result, but it does shine a spotlight on just how hard it can be to manage financially during what should be a wonderful time for a young family.

Finances as kids grow

Childcare is just one piece of the family finance budget. According to Jess, couples should consider laying out all their expenses in a budget for the years to come. 'When you start considering your budget in terms of holidays, cars and properties, you start to see how much you have left, or in fact, don't have.'

Jess suggests, if you can, you might look into investing early on in your family life together. The amount you invest is inevitably 'budget permitting', but it's particularly helpful if you intend to not only provide paid care for your children, but as you look beyond their early years to education. This is why financial planners encourage their clients to look long-term, not just at the immediate costs in front of them. Living year to year and trying to cover both the cost of living and all of the expenses that come with having children does require you to do some honest forecasting based on your circumstances and what you want for your life as a family.

Couple goals check-in

Having children is a goal that no one wants to put a price on, but being prepared can have a huge impact on the quality of the early years of your life as a family. Have you thought about these questions?

- Do we want children?
- If we struggle to conceive, will we do IVF?
- Do we know how much it costs and how many rounds we would be prepared to do?
- Who will take time out of the workforce to care for the child/children?
- What impact will this have on our careers?
- Do we know how much it costs to have a baby and are we financially prepared?
- Would we consider splitting superannuation between the working and non-working partner during parental leave?
- What are our essential and non-essential purchases during pregnancy and parental leave?
- How will we pay for childcare and early education?
- Will we choose private or public schools?

CHAPTER ELEVEN

Wills, inheritance and insurance

Like most people, I'm so busy thinking about how to get through a day, week or year, I don't stop to think about what happens in the event of my death, which has probably been for the best given how reckless I've been at some points in my life. It's remarkable that my liver's still going considering what I've put it through.

Even when I bought my house, I did think, well, I guess my family will just sell it and divvy up any profits in the event that something happens to me. I didn't anticipate anyone else making a claim and I've never really thought about my stuff as an 'estate'. In my mind, an estate was a huge property with manicured lawns and box hedges along the perimeter. But when you die, you have an estate, and if you die without a will, you're what's known as 'intestate', which means that the relevant laws that govern your state or territory will dictate what happens to your belongings. You needn't be rich to have an estate – the contents of your bank accounts, superannuation, car and even your pets are considered to be valuable items that must find a new home.

It wasn't something I started to take seriously until Sam showed up. What would happen to the house if my number was up? Would it become his? Who should get my superannuation and any other savings I might have at that time?

How should I decide?

Money aside, I don't want those I leave behind to be worrying about this stuff when they're – presumably – grieving my untimely passing. So, I decided it was really time to do something about it.

My situation was still relatively straightforward as long as there were no children to consider, but for people with kids, a will is arguably essential if you don't want the legal system to manage your estate. While the implications vary from state to state, your partner generally stands to be the biggest beneficiary if you die intestate – whether you've been married for decades or you're in a more recent de-facto arrangement.

I was stunned to learn that more than 60 per cent of Australians die intestate. Why do so few people take the time to draw up a will? First, it's perceived to be expensive. Second, most people don't love dedicating time to mortality-related admin and then forking out for the legal costs.

Until recently, one of the most affordable alternatives to seeking out a lawyer was grabbing a will kit from the post office. However, industry experts say will kits are often filled out without legal review and a lot of people mess them up, even though they intend to have a legally binding will.

A traditional will that is drawn up with bespoke legal advice can cost at least $1,000 and sometimes a lot more depending on the complexity. In recent years new companies have begun disrupting the end-of-life industry with flat-rate wills documented for less than $200, attracting people who know they need to get this task done but don't want to blow their savings on it.

These services don't provide bespoke legal advice but there are prompts throughout the process delivered by their legal team. They make sure that you've used the platform correctly and that your document is valid.

When people die, there is a legal document that confirms that a will is valid and can be acted on. This is known as probate. When you have a will the process of obtaining probate means you have specified how your estate should be administered. Without a will, it's open to interpretation and contestation because you haven't specified those things.

Importantly, having a will allows you to appoint an executor. That's someone who will be responsible for the administration associated with dividing your estate in accordance with what you've set out in the will.

In the case of complex situations, people may need bespoke legal advice to ensure that family members are adequately considered. That's not just financial, anyone with children will likely have specific guardianship wishes and want to ensure their children's living, social and emotional needs are met.

Entering a relationship with children

Estate planning becomes absolutely imperative when you have kids. Whether you have children in a present relationship or are bringing children from a previous relationship into a new one, their future wellbeing in the event that something happens to you is likely your biggest priority.

CASE STUDY

Forty-six-year-old Melbourne-based Anita met her husband through family about twelve years ago. Anita's husband had two children from a previous relationship, and they have one son together. Given Anita's husband had two children and the value of the assets they brought to their relationship was quite different, Anita says it was 'very important' to have a formal agreement drawn up so that both they and their children would be protected if anything happened.

'My husband was open to this discussion; we are both pragmatic about these things,' she says. It was Anita who instigated the process. 'He understood where I was coming from and was happy to formally address it,' she recalls.

To arrange the legal documents, they engaged a lawyer to draft their wills. 'This was an interesting process. Sitting in his office and going over various scenarios surrounding our mortality was quite confronting and comical at the same time,' Anita says.

Indeed, it definitely helps to laugh about scenarios that you don't ever want to be faced with. Anita's key concern was financial. 'What would happen to our family home? How would the value upon sale be divided up between the three kids?' Anita wondered. It was particularly complex because Anita had come to the relationship with more money initially, so they had to find a fair way for any possible inheritance for the children to be divided.

Anita and her husband both have their own individual wills, and each will has two trustees. 'They were chosen based on the family and friendship connections and the trust we have in these people,' Anita says.

Anita's experience is a best-case scenario, as her husband was so willing to engage in the legal and financial requirements needed to make these essential decisions, but she understands that not all couples find estate planning easy or desirable, and that sometimes one or both parties will be anxious about tackling these issues. Her advice to couples in her situation? 'Communication is key – be open and honest with your partner and focus on the best outcomes for the children.'

Finally, bespoke legal advice is not something that people look forward to paying for, but it is arguably an invaluable investment. 'Get the support from a good lawyer who can guide you through the process and also suggest things you may not have thought of,' Anita says.

According to family lawyer Laura Vickers, many couples will arrange their estate plan to leave some of their money and assets to their partner and their children. This is to avoid a will challenge, but also because most people in this situation want to make sure both are provided for.

'If you leave everything to one or the other, there is no guarantee that your children will receive anything from that partner when he or she dies, or vice versa,' Laura says.

Here are some examples of distribution of assets that protect your loved ones equally:

- Owning your home as tenants in common, giving your spouse a 'life interest' in your half of the home when you die, and then your half going to your kids when your spouse dies and/or re-partners and/or doesn't want to live there any more

- Leaving your share of your home to your partner but a portion of your super or life insurance to your kids
- Leaving one property to your spouse and another to your child.

But Laura cautions, an estate plan can only be effective if the assets have 'the correct ownership structure as any assets that are owned as joint tenants will automatically go to the other joint tenant if one of you dies. This bypasses the will and makes any clause in there directing it to a third party ineffective, and this applies not only to properties but bank accounts too.'

You also need to make sure that your superannuation nomination lines up with your estate plan. If your will says your super should go to your partner, but your binding death benefit nomination directs it to your dependent child or your estate, the nomination will prevail.

Ultimately, you need to think about what you want the result to be after you die and ensure that your assets are owned in a way that lines up with your estate plan.

If you don't have a will, and you have children from a previous relationship and a new partner, the consequences could be dire for your kids. According to Laura's estate lawyer colleague, Marlee Viero, in the state of Victoria, for example, your partner could receive all of your valuables, a lump sum starting at about $451,000 (adjusted for CPI and interest), plus 50 per cent of the balance of your estate. Your children then get the remaining 50 per cent. 'If you have less than $451,000 in assets, it all goes to the partner.' That's potentially not much going to your offspring, and the bulk going to someone that you may love but have only been with for a few years. But in Tasmania, for example, the amount is $350,000, so if you die without a will but leave assets in different states, you will have two different formulas applied.

It gets even more complicated if you have more than one partner. In some circumstances, being separated but not yet divorced, while also having a new partner, means there are two people to consider. Alternatively, people may have more than one relationship taking place at the time of their passing.

How much should you leave to your children?

Laura explains that the amount left to children will depend on whether your children are from your present relationship or whether you're a blended family. She says most couples in non-blended families with no kids from a previous relationship leave everything to each other. 'This is because in that situation, the surviving spouse would often be needing every cent to pay off debt and raise the kids.'

That said, some people might be concerned that if they die, their spouse could enter a new relationship and their kids' inheritance could be at risk of a family law dispute with the new partner. In such cases, some people 'section off some of their assets' that go into a trust for which their kids are beneficiaries. Additionally, that trust is not controlled solely by their spouse. They may also take out a life insurance policy purely for the benefit of their children.

Of course, it's not just the money and obvious assets that you need to consider. You also might consider whether you want to leave emotionally meaningful items such as jewellery or artwork to a particular child.

It's important to understand the ramifications if you leave significantly unequal amounts to each child. In such a case, regardless of your reason for doing so, you need to ensure you're 'creating evidence outside of the will to help defend a challenge that one child should have received more'.

Also – this might sound obvious – your will can't pass on ownership of an asset that you don't own. For example, perhaps a wife owns a business and the family home's title is in her husband's name, so if she's sued the property isn't at risk. When he dies, the property will go into a testamentary trust set up by his will. Her name is on the mortgage, because her borrowing capacity was needed for the home loan application. She would need to sign a document for the bank confirming she had received independent legal advice about the risks of this arrangement, as she would be liable for the debt even though she doesn't own the property.

When should kids get access to their inheritance?

Imagine leaving your kids a huge lump sum only for them to blow it all. Perhaps you wouldn't begrudge them dropping a few grand on good times if that makes them happy. Perhaps that money allows them to take some time out of work to properly grieve and take care of themselves. But let's say you're in the fortunate position to leave a young person hundreds of thousands of dollars. When should they get access to it?

The standard is twenty-one but some couples realise their young adult offspring mightn't be financially mature enough to manage money at that age, so they up the age of access to twenty-five or even thirty. According to Laura, 'Others might include a mechanism in the trust that allows a "financial apprenticeship" for a period of years, managing money under the watchful eye of the trustee.'

Who cares for your children if you die?

If your children have another living parent at the time of your death, whether you're in a relationship or not, they will be the default testamentary guardian. The testamentary guardian is responsible for your children's daily and long-term needs. You can add a co-guardian to act jointly with them if the will maker is concerned they aren't capable of doing the job by themselves.

The testamentary guardian isn't always the person that the child lives with, but they are the one authorised to make decisions about living arrangements (subject to a family court order). If you are in a position to think about guardians who may be appointed in addition to any surviving parent, there are many human qualities and practical factors to consider.

First, and perhaps the most crucial: Do you trust the person to raise your child the way you want them to be raised? You need to think about their parenting style, values and beliefs because although you can be quite prescriptive in the guidance you provide in your written wishes, you're obviously not going to be there to oversee things. That means the guardian should ideally intrinsically share your broad views on how a young person should be raised.

Next, it's one thing to choose someone you believe will play a pivotal role in raising your kids, but it's another to have them truly want to do it. The person must be 'willing and physically able' to perform the guardian role, Laura tells me, and highlights an example where a guardian may consider having children of their own or more if they already have some. In that instance, will they still have the energy and time to devote to raising your child? That's not necessarily always going to be the case, but something to bear in mind nonetheless.

Practical considerations include where the prospective guardian lives and how old they are. In terms of their location, do you want your child to be relocated? Moving could be really hard on your child. When it comes to age, you can amend your will if your intended guardian later becomes unable to provide adequate care due to age or physical inability. Additionally, you may appoint your parents until they reach a certain age, at which point guardianship moves to a sibling or friend.

What's the difference between a guardian and a trustee?

While the guardian is responsible for caring for and raising children, the trustee takes the lead on managing the inheritance until the kids reach the nominated age at which they're allowed to access their trust and take full control of it. Laura has seen some clients name one person as both the guardian and the trustee if that's the only person they trust to care for their children. Trust – particularly when it comes to choosing someone who won't be pressured by others to misuse any funds – is critical in your decision-making.

However, there are risks associated with leaving both roles to one person because there's no one independent keeping an eye on how the guardian is managing money intended for the children. 'If the roles are split, the trustee would advance funds from the estate to be used for, say, education expenses and would make sure they are applied for that purpose,' Laura explains.

A trustee's role can span decades

According to estate lawyer Marlee Viero, if a trustee begins their role when children are young, and they aren't given access to their inheritance when they're adults, that's a long commitment, particularly when the will states that the children don't receive control until well into adulthood.

That means the trustee must manage the child or children's finances associated with their trust (which is where the kids' inheritance is held) for a considerable period of time. Just some of the responsibilities include: opening a bank account for the trust, lodging the trust's bank tax return each year and providing funds from the trust for education, medical and living expenses as needed. They also have to manage negotiations with the kids when they're over the age of eighteen, but they haven't reached the 'vesting age' (vesting being the point that they're able to access their inheritance and associated assets).

Finally, the trustee is always required to do their due diligence and get professional financial and tax advice when investing funds held on behalf of the children.

What happens if a former partner or family members contest a will?

Nothing quite brings out people's true colours like a robust contest over a will. The combination of money and perceived fairness – and sometimes just straight-up greed – will do that. But according to the experts, before anyone can contest a will and bring a challenge, they need legal advice and the lawyer will tell them if it's worth their time. The reality is, sometimes legal fees make a contest pointless: i.e.

you're unlikely to spend thousands contesting the rightful ownership of your grandparents' cutlery set unless it holds some significant value to you, and you can justify the spend.

But, if the claim is something that a family member really wants to go ahead with, it could be game on. A challenge can be based on the fact that a proper provision was not made for that person under the will. Laura says, 'This can be argued by spouses or former partners, minor or financially dependent children or step-children, grandchildren or financial dependents.'

In short: a lot of people can come after your estate and if they can't reach a settlement, they're off to court, which is expensive and time-consuming, not to mention emotionally draining for those involved, especially in a time of grief.

How to prevent a challenge

All wills can be challenged, but there are things you can do to prevent this from happening. There are a couple of options if you want to ensure your wishes are carried out as planned. First, if you can, see that your will provides for everyone that it should. Having said that, there are many cases where this isn't feasible. For example, maybe you're estranged from your child or your parents – it happens. What then?

Or, if you have remarried and you want to ensure your former partner doesn't have access to your estate, here are some things you can do to ensure your assets can't be contested:

Use 'joint tenant' ownership structures

If a property or bank accounts are held jointly with someone else, the share of that asset or money is passed to the other person when someone dies. By contrast, if a property is owned only in one name, future ownership is open to being contested.

Nominating superannuation beneficiaries

In most cases, superannuation is not covered in your will. It is held by the trustee of the super fund. You need to proactively make arrangements with your super fund to appoint your beneficiaries to make sure it ends up with the people you want to have it. Beneficiaries can be your partner or spouse, your children, anyone who is financially dependent on you, or the executor of your will. Importantly, the nominee can't be anyone you feel like choosing. They either need to be a spouse, your child, an interdependent (that's someone who lives with you that you might provide domestic support or personal care to) or someone who's financially dependent. In my case, Sam was the only valid nomination. This is why a supporting estate plan is important if you also want other family members to receive a portion of your estate in the event of your death.

You will be able to access the required forms through your superannuation provider. Be mindful that some beneficiaries lapse, so you need to keep the information up to date. Similarly, if you nominate a partner, split up with them and begin a relationship with someone else, your ex-partner is still the beneficiary until you make the change.

Gifting your assets

Finally, there's nothing stopping you from gifting parts of your estate before you die, if you have the opportunity and desire to do so. You can do this simply by giving cash, jewellery, art or cars to the people you love. You may also transfer shares or property ownership, but in these scenarios, there may be capital gains taxes that apply, so it's worth speaking to a personal finance expert if you are in the fortunate position to be gifting shares or property.

That said, gifting reduces the amount in your estate that is subject to being challenged. If you don't want to provide for someone but can't restructure your estate, Laura says you can write up 'affidavits to back up your reasoning for leaving your estate as you have. These could be used as evidence in court if a claim arose post-death.'

She encourages people to think beyond a will to holistic estate planning as an estate plan is much more than a will. This is because it includes an enduring power of attorney, who can make decisions if you or your partner lose capacity. It also includes a superannuation nomination, which we've discussed, and a 'memorandum of wishes' which allows you to get really specific with your trustee and any guardians you appoint to look after your children.

How much to insure

Forking out for insurance has often felt like a grudge-spend for me. Like, the cost of living is so high, I also have to dish out some of my hard-earned coin for something that *might* happen? Come on. But according to Rebecca Pritchard, when people say they can't afford insurance, she argues, 'You can't afford not to have insurance.' In other words, the people who don't have a lot of spare funds on hand need it the most.

It's critical for all couples to have conversations about what's required to adequately insure their lives. All too often, mortgages and kids are the motivators for getting it. Additionally, what I'd describe as the *big* protection investments – life insurance and Total and Permanent Disability (TPD) insurance, trauma insurance and income protection insurance – are often perceived to be for 'older' people, but in fact according to Rebecca, 'The best time to get insurance is when you're young, before things start breaking down in your body.' That's because most people have pre-existing conditions by the time they get around to locking in personal insurance.

She adds, 'Very few people in their thirties and forties don't have at least one exclusion.' An exclusion is a pre-existing medical condition or circumstance that means you can't make a claim. For example, a history of substance abuse may be an exclusion. If you work in a dangerous job, that could also have an impact on your exclusions. So if you can get insurance at twenty-five and don't have any exclusions, that's likely going to be better for your premium.

In terms of deciding what to cover, the best approach is to entertain some 'what-if' scenarios. For example, perhaps you're renting, but you want to know if something happened to one of you, the other could buy a house.

To work out how much people actually need to insure, Rebecca uses an 'Insurance Needs Analysis', which helps couples to work out which specific risks are relevant to their life and then develop an insurance strategy around it. Importantly this is not something you do once and forget about. Your insurance needs will change as your life evolves and should be reviewed at regular intervals, particularly if you're taking on significant debt, having children, selling an asset or you have a change in income.

But how much is a life worth? Are you worth a million dollars? More? You don't just pluck a random insurance number out of nowhere. That's where Insurance Needs Analysis comes in.

If you die or become permanently disabled, here are some things you might consider. These numbers will of course depend on your circumstances, but they are common costs that financial planners and insurers will consider:

Reason for claim	Things to cover	Example amount
Death	Clear debt (house, cars) Funeral & other costs Leave partner with two years of income	$500,000 $25,000 $80,000 x 2 years ($160,000 total) Total death cover: $685,000
Total and permanent disability (TPD)	Clear debt (house, cars) Higher care facility bond Carer expenses for 25 years	$500,000 $200,000 $530,000 Total TPD cover: $1,230,000

How does insurance impact your cashflow?

While I can't tell you what your insurance should cost you, I will say it could be a pretty negligible amount in the context of how much it protects you and your family in the event of a traumatic event. Sam and I now have comprehensive insurance that covers the kinds of claims listed in the table above. Most of the costs come out of our superannuation and a small portion of the balance comes out of our cashflow. As Sam said when he saw the impact on our cashflow, 'We spend more on streaming services each month.' All in all, it's a small price to pay for the peace of mind we get in return.

Couple goals check-in

Few people want to talk about this stuff – me included. But you don't want to leave your loved ones in a position where they're battling over your assets if something happens to you. Here are some points to talk about if you're considering estate planning and insurance.

- Do we have an adequate will?
- Have we discussed who cares for our children if we're unable to?
- Is our superannuation nomination up to date?
- Do we have adequate insurance?
- Are we likely to have an inheritance to pass on?
- Who will receive our assets when we die?

CHAPTER TWELVE

Fighting for FIRE (Financial Independence, Retire Early)

For many of us, our biggest couple goal is a comfortable retirement. Depending on your age, that might seem so distant that it's impossible to work out how you'll do it, but there's a growing informal push, both in Australia and around the world, known as the Financial Independence, Retire Early (FIRE) movement that challenges the common belief that we should work full-time, get a mortgage and schlep to and from the office for most of adulthood until we own our homes and can survive on any remaining savings, superannuation and the pension.

Those who subscribe to FIRE are working, sometimes quite aggressively, to meet savings and investing targets early in their professional lives, so that they can kick back and relax well before they turn sixty-five.

CASE STUDY

Ana Kresina, who's in her thirties, is committed to FIRE. She was fortunate to grow up in a family that prioritised saving over spending and set her up with good habits early in life. Originally from Canada, she began contributing to the Canadian equivalent of superannuation and also a tax-free savings account, both of which invested customers' funds in the stock market to deliver a return.

'What I didn't understand at the time was how it worked. I just knew it was a thing you should do. But since I was on a lower income, I would only squirrel away a little bit here and there,' Ana says. Later, Ana bought an apartment in Canada using the equivalent of Australia's First-Home Super Saver Scheme and got a roommate in to help keep her costs manageable while she prioritised paying the mortgage down.

In 2014, Ana moved to Australia and accepted a role with a tech company that paid 50 per cent more than she'd been earning in Canada and her frugal nature enabled her to save large portions of her salary. At that time, she believed the best thing to do with her excess funds was to continue to pay down the mortgage on her Canada apartment. 'I knew that investing was a way to build wealth, but everyone I talked to about it thought it was gambling, so I really didn't know where to start,' Ana says. So, she took to the internet and came across the Mr Money Moustache blog, run by Canadian-born former software engineer Peter Adeny, who'd retired from his job in 2005, aged thirty. He'd achieved this by living on a small portion of his salary and investing everything else in the stock market and index funds.

'After reading about the simple concept, I was hooked. I realised I already had the initial savings mentality but the part I was missing out on was the investing side of things,' Ana says, so she began consuming FIRE content and researching what to invest in. Initially she was a bit overwhelmed as she came to terms with concepts including risk, diversification and asset allocation. In the end, 'I ended up making the best-calculated choice and invested in exchange traded funds [ETFs],' Ana says, though admits she was scared to invest in one ETF in one lump sum, which is why she bought several. She's since become more sophisticated in her investing decisions but says simply starting gave her motivation she needed to keep going. 'I was massively relieved that I just did something, even if I was still learning. Analysis paralysis is a real thing.'

Ana's commitment to investing and achieving FIRE began before she met her partner. 'I wanted to have kids and was considering IVF as a single person. Knowing how expensive fertility treatment can be, it was something I was factoring into my financial goals along with the cost of medical treatment for endometriosis and having children too.'

Initially, Ana and her partner were friends and they talked openly about their financial goals. 'I saw we were aligned despite being at different parts of our journey,' she says. This was important to her as she'd previously dated people who spent mindlessly and this was a concern as she thought about the reality of having children and a home.

While Ana and her partner supported one another wholeheartedly, they kept their finances separate until they bought a property together, which was after their first child was born. 'Even now, some of our assets are separate, and my FIRE goals and tracking are separate from his.'

But having separate financial goals doesn't mean they're not good together. 'My partner is my biggest cheerleader and supporter of my goals, both financially and otherwise,' Ana says. Indeed, there are many things that make them a good team beyond money. The pair are equally responsible for school drop-offs and pick-ups, they share parenting equally when they are both working and both do their share of household chores.

The goal is for both Ana and her partner to retire early, but they are at different stages on their individual financial paths. For example, Ana says, 'I am further along in my career, have a higher wage and am more senior in my role.' Because she started her FIRE plan young, she also has more assets. 'So although our mentality of spending less, saving more and investing is aligned, chances are I will reach FIRE first,' she says. 'Something that I've always valued is independence and autonomy. And to have that, I need some kind of financial security. I've never wanted to rely on another person for financial security – especially not a partner, and especially not a man,' Ana says. This is in part due to seeing her parents' traditionally gendered relationship. 'I never wanted to be in a situation where I couldn't leave a bad relationship due to money,' she adds.

Setting your FIRE goal

It's essential to note that you can set a FIRE goal with or without a partner. In the case study above, Ana is proceeding with her FIRE goals independently of her partner.

You can run a few equations to establish your FIRE number based on Lean FI, Regular FI or Fat FI. In the case of Lean FI, for example, you're calculating your bare minimum to live on. If you're striving for Fat FI, you're effectively building in some fat – allowing for holidays and other luxuries.

To reach the number, you need to work out what you would need to live on to cover your expense and lifestyle annually for the number of years you intend to retire or live off the dividends from your investments.

The foundations of the maths to achieve FIRE is based on the Trinity study, which was published in 1998 by three finance professors at Trinity University. The paper aimed to establish reliable withdrawal rates from share portfolios, allowing for growth and shrinkage based on market activity (i.e. share prices rising and falling over time). The idea was that a portfolio, when withdrawn from safely, could last for the duration of a person's retirement.

Ultimately that safe withdrawal rate was deemed to be 4 per cent in the first year (and adjusted for inflation after that), removing the risk of running out of money for decades. In simple terms, if you retire with $1 million, your 4 per cent withdrawal in the first year is $40,000.

In our case study above, Ana based her calculations on $60,000 a year in income, which made the rough FIRE number $1.5 million ($60,000 x 25 = $1.5 million). Ana counted all of the funds she has in investments that would become the money required to help her live with complete financial independence.

To calculate this, she did not include:

- Her principal place of residence (i.e. her family home)
- The funds in her offset account (this is money allocated for her principal place of residence)
- Superannuation and the retirement fund she still holds in Canada.

The funds in her FIRE assets *do* include:

- Money invested in her taxable brokerage accounts and her tax-free savings account in Canada
- The value of her investment property in Canada.

Some people might not include the value of an investment property and only include the rental income derived from it, but Ana sold the property recently, so some of the proceeds became part of her total FIRE assets.

Allowing for life, families and reality

Ana was clever in making some serious headway before she had children, because projections for reaching FIRE might as well go in the bin when you're factoring family in.

As we know, money is never just money. Values and emotions drive much of any couple's financial decision-making. You might be happy in a small two-bedroom apartment in the city but children change everything. You might want more space and more bedrooms in a different neighbourhood. As we discussed in the chapter on kids, the reality is: the cost of small children, coupled with income loss due to parental leave, is brutal. It's an entire change of lifestyle.

Having a family has changed Ana's view on the pace required to achieve her FIRE goals. She's now working to build a bigger emergency fund and the couple are discussing whether they should focus on paying down more of their mortgage before returning to an investing focus.

Ana admits that it would be cheaper in the short-term to rent but says 'security for our family was very important to us. The truth is, if you own a principal place of residence, it is an asset that isn't generating any income. But it provides stability, and indeed everyone needs a place to live.'

Housing is a big factor, because FIRE focuses on assets that generate income, but without a home, it is much harder to anticipate how much you'll need to live on each year – and the cost of living will inevitably be much higher for a couple who have to factor in rent and the possibility of regular moving costs than a couple who own their home when they exit the workforce.

The whole point of FIRE is to have investments that grow in value – both through capital gains and through dividend payment. That way, when you do retire, your investments will generate an income for you. And although that could be true of property, it's not as liquid, and it doesn't generate income (unless rented out).

The numbers required to achieve FIRE can be daunting, but a permanant early retirement doesn't have to be the goal, a suitable lifestyle can be just as attractive. Ana hopes that in time she'll obtain the financial independence component. This involves making work optional rather than mandatory, and having an abundance of time to spend with her partner and children. 'Really it's about having the time and freedom to do what I want, when I want.'

In telling Ana's story, I don't want to create undue anxiety. Working towards a goal of owning a home and having $1.5 million in dividend-paying assets on top of superannuation is a remarkable aspiration, but it's not for everyone and that's okay. The point here is to simply get you thinking about the reality of what retirement, or even a reduced dependence on working, might cost depending on your values and lifestyle goals. Ana repeatedly acknowledged her privilege in our discussion.

What's important is that she not only knows what she wants, she knows what it's going to cost. 'Another thing that I think helps is having actual data – showing projections from a compound interest calculator, or other stats, is a great way to visualise wealth in the future,' she says.

Finally, Ana says whatever you want your retirement to look like, it's never too early to start discussing this as a couple. 'I've found being open about what I am trying to achieve and what my values are is a good place to start. That way you can build on those goals and aspirations and create a plan that you can work on together.'

Should you calculate your net worth?

Some personal finance experts like to use net worth as an indicator of financial health. Others see it as an unreliable figure that can change over time. For example, a significant portion of your net wealth may be comprised of home equity and superannuation, but in an economic downturn, the value of your home may drop and the share market could take a hit, in turn impacting your super.

Your net worth gives you a broad picture of what you've built so far. But net worth doesn't generate much in terms of day-to-day cashflow, unless you have a sizable share portfolio that delivers passive income in the form of dividends, or you refinance your home to turn equity into cash.

Still, as a couple, it could be useful to complete a net-worth exercise to see how your assets and liabilities stack up when your individual positions are combined. Running these numbers can be a useful motivator.

Calculating your net worth

In simple terms, net worth is the calculation of all of your assets, minus your liabilities. You can find a net worth calculator at moneysmart.gov.au.

Net wealth gives you two key insights:

- Whether or not your assets outweigh your debts
- A view of your current overall financial health

Here are the key inputs when you calculate your net worth:

Assets	Liabilities
Home value	Mortgage
Additional properties/ land	Personal loans
Superannuation	Car loans
Trusts	Investment loans
Shares	HECS debt
Other investments	Credit card debt
Savings	Hire/purchase
Value of business	Interest-free loans
Cars, boats, caravans	Business loans

Combine your totals to generate a shared net wealth position and input each figure into the calculator to see where you land together. So, for example, if one of you has $90,000 in superannuation and the other has $50,000, you'll input $140,000 in the superannuation field. You mightn't have a figure for every possible asset or liability. Simply include the ones that are relevant to you.

Here's an example in which I've combined a couple's total assets and liabilities:

Assets	Shared total	Liabilities	Shared total
Home value	$650,000	Mortgage	$470,000
Cars, boats, caravans (total value)	$20,000	Car loans owing	$15,000
Shares	$5,000	Personal loans	$3,000
Savings	$10,000	Credit card debt	$1,000
Superannuation	$140,000	Business loans	$7,500
Total assets	**$825,000**	**Total liabilities**	**$496,500**
		Total net worth	$328,500

Bringing it all together to plan for your future

With a clear view of your current net wealth, you can see where you are today, and what you need to do to achieve your retirement goals. Your financial aspiration will, as we've discussed previously, depend on what you want your ideal lifestyle to look like. If you want to own a modest home, and don't plan to travel internationally or indulge in a lavish lifestyle, you may be quite comfortable with the age pension and some superannuation. But if you're forecasting cocktails and cruises in your eighties, you're probably going to want to secure more assets that provide passive income to support such a lifestyle. Either way, what is the golden figure you should be working towards?

Super Consumers Australia's retirement saving targets might help you to work out how much additional super you should have. Their figures are based on how much super you'll need to have at retirement to supplement the age pension. Here are the current figures for pre-retirees aged fifty-five to sixty-nine. These numbers assume you own your home outright. If you're younger and don't have a home, don't panic, we'll talk about that shortly.

If you own your own home when you retire and you live	And you'd like to spend this much in retirement	Then you need to have saved this much by sixty-five
By yourself	**Low** $1,308 per fortnight $34,000 per year	$88,000
By yourself	**Medium** $1,692 per fortnight $44,000 per year	$301,000
By yourself	**High** $2,115 per fortnight $55,000 per year	$745,000
In a couple	**Low** $1,846 per fortnight $48,000 per year	$111,000
In a couple	**Medium** $2,462 per fortnight $64,000 per year	$402,000
In a couple	**High** $3,115 per fortnight $81,000 per year	$1,003,000

Now is the best time to start thinking about retirement

According to Rebecca Pritchard, you should ideally start planning for retirement today. It might seem like giving up work is a distant dream, but the best asset you have is time.

The question, inevitably, is how much do you really need in retirement? How can anyone predict how much their life is going to cost ten, twenty or thirty years from now? The answer is to look at your lifestyle now and revisit your long-term vision. This brings us back to cashflow. You can't work out how much you'll need if you don't know what it costs to live your life.

Of course, what your life costs now will look different when it comes time to live a life of leisure, but there are some variables you can consider. Will you own your home? Or will you have an investment portfolio that supplements your income on top of the age pension?

Then there are other discretionary lifestyle choices. Are you happy to stay at home and tend to your garden? Will you play golf? Do you want an annual international holiday and enough money to spoil your grandchildren if you have them?

A key priority for many people is to own their home. If you have a house paid off, that reduces your expenses, because you're not paying for rent or a mortgage. In turn, that means you need less income than someone who has ongoing housing costs. 'Studies show financial security is at its strongest if you own a property in retirement,' Rebecca says. But these studies reflect what has traditionally been done for many years, particularly by the Baby Boomers, many of whom have set up comfortable retirements through property ownership. Given the cost of property, that's simply not an option for everyone. This is perhaps why young people are turning to alternative ways to build wealth. According to the *Australian Financial Review*, in 2021, nearly 300,000 people made their first investment in the share market, and most of them were millennials.

It will be interesting to see how future generations of retirees handle their retirement. Millennials and Generation Z are facing much lower levels of home ownership in retirement due to the fact that it is becoming exceedingly difficult to enter the market at all. So what else will the next generation do to generate the money needed for a comfortable retirement? That 'something else' would need to be investing in assets that deliver a return in the same manner that property can – shares, for example. However, for those who choose to build a healthy share portfolio rather than a bricks and mortar asset, housing is still going to be a consideration. God knows what it'll cost to rent a house in 2060 …

Once you've decided what you want to prioritise – whether that be housing, shares, super or something else – you then need to establish how long you both intend to work for. Rebecca believes you might be surprised when you start 'demystifying assumptions'. Perhaps until now you've just figured you'll both work until you're about sixty-five, maybe seventy. But if you have the conversation, one of you might say, 'I love my job and I plan to work until the day I die.' The other might say, 'I want to be out the door at fifty-five.'

With this information, you can make adjustments to your plan based on a firmer idea of how many working years you have left to achieve your goals. Your present situation will also dictate what you do with the spare funds that you do have to put towards your retirement. You might think you need to put more money into super but there are alternatives to additional voluntary contributions.

To work out what's best for you, you need to look at where your surplus funds will have the most impact. For example, if you're planning a family or raising children, it mightn't make sense to put more money into superannuation (over and above the compulsory amount) at this point; perhaps you need that money for a house deposit, or for school fees. In this case you might think about staggering your financial goals and putting money into investments that have more liquidity in the short-term. A licensed financial professional can help you work out what's best for both your present and future circumstances.

What happens if you don't own a home when you retire?

There's little doubt that the concept of retirement is going to change dramatically as more and more Australians reach retirement age without a home. But if you're young enough to have been accumulating superannuation from a young age, your future may look brighter than you think. I used the MoneySmart retirement planner to get a sense of how retirement income is calculated. If you want to try this yourself, go to moneysmart.gov.au and you can plug in your age, your income and your current super balance, along with the same information from your partner, to see how much annual income you could generate between the two of you.

It's a model, rather than an accurate prediction, because it doesn't account for how much money you'll make in the years to come, your personal circumstances, tax or inflation. But for me, simply taking a look at this tool was a strong reminder that superannuation will likely make a huge difference to the comfort levels of upcoming generations, compared to those who didn't have it.

If you're investing elsewhere on top of superannuation, that could also boost your comfort levels. Couples, it seems, are also great at keeping themselves accountable and motivated. Sarah King from online investment company Stockspot says their firm has seen joint investment account holders top up 25 per cent more than individual account holders.

'The benefits of investing jointly is that you'll typically have a larger amount of money to invest at the outset because you're joining forces. You can top up with a larger amount each week or month or as regularly as you like,' she adds.

CASE STUDY

Sydney-based Fayme and Miguel have chosen a wealth-building strategy that doesn't include purchasing a home. The pair celebrated their ten-year wedding anniversary in 2022. Fayme, who works in health, and Miguel, who is in financial services, say 'buying a house doesn't stack up' for them.

They say there are a few reasons for this. 'We think investing is better than buying a house to diversify the use of our capital. Then there's the opportunity cost. What are we sacrificing if we buy a house?' Fayme and Miguel have wondered.

From a set-up perspective, it's cost them far less to invest. It cost them nothing to set up a brokerage account. They invest in low-cost index funds and the management fees deducted are 0.08 per cent of their total portfolio. They spend approximately $10 per fortnight in brokerage fees when they add to their portfolio – a total of $260 per year.

'Compare that to the cost of buying a house, setting up a mortgage, bank interest, legal fees, building inspections and ongoing maintenance costs,' Miguel says. Additionally, they value flexibility. While they acknowledge that the security of home ownership is important to others, 'Not buying a house allows us to move when we want, downgrade or upgrade our shelter of choice, live interstate or overseas if we want to,' Fayme says.

Currently, their plan is to be life-long renters. 'If our investments eventually cover our rent [via passive income], we see that as the same as being mortgage free,' Miguel says. They describe their investment strategy as 'quite boring', with an allocation of 50 per cent Australian, 30 per cent US and the remaining 20 per cent invested in other companies around the world. 'There's no higher-order reasoning behind this,' he says. 'We top up our portfolio regularly into broad-based index ETFs, ensuring that the allocation is re-balanced close to the desired allocation. Our regular top-up amount is 30 per cent of our combined income, and a lump sum top-up from time to time if we have excess funds from dividends or a surplus that exceeds our cash buffers.'

Given how much they're investing, Fayme and Miguel believe they're on track to live a comfortable retirement without a home. They've made conservative calculations that indicate that even if they never added another dollar to their portfolio, they'd have

75 per cent of their current annual incomes (in today's dollars) available to them every year from the ages of sixty-five to 100. 'We only use these projections as a loose gauge of our progress and we know for a fact that real life is not lived through a spreadsheet,' Fayme says.

Housing-wise, they have secured a rental in a build-to-rent property where they have long-term stability. Build-to-rent developments usually remain owned by the developer, and often have more flexible lease conditions. In Fayme and Miguel's case, they were able to lock in their rent at a fixed rate from 2022 to 2024. 'Being exposed to build-to-rent, we are somewhat optimistic about our future options. These models give us hope that these industries will compete with the traditional rental model and provide alternative housing options for renters.'

'Not owning a home in retirement is fine by us,' they say, pointing out that they don't necessarily want to be mowing the lawn, cleaning gutters or doing renovations. 'Our ideal retirement involves being close to parks, public transport, lifestyle, entertainment and healthcare facilities. We want the ability to have someone else fix and upgrade what is required so we can maximise our time travelling, exploring new hobbies and eating out.'

Right now, Fayme and Miguel are happy to be living as they choose and travelling as they please without being tied to the commitment of bricks and mortar. 'At the same time, we are forward-thinking in our strategy to look after our future selves by ensuring that we have enough income-producing assets to fund not only our housing but also our lifestyle when we decide to retire.'

The future of retirement

While most of the experts I consulted advocated for thinking seriously about retirement as early as you possibly can, it's a long way off for many of us. And I don't want you getting too worked up about what the future holds.

Many predictions also indicate that retirement will likely look very different in the years to come. We're living much longer than we once did. In the early 1990s, the average life expectancy was about seventy-four years for men and eighty years for women. By 2021, it had blown out to an average of eighty years for men and eighty-five years for women. When you're nearing retirement, it could be much higher. If you're fortunate, at the age of sixty-five you'll still be positively sprightly. So if you retire at that point and live until you're 100, what are you going to do for *thirty-five* years? I suspect many of us will do things that generate income, but we'll do it on our terms. We'll be innovating, creating, logging into our emails (or whatever the equivalent is in a few decades) from remote locations, tinkering with tasks at our convenience, and doing them because we also get some enjoyment out of the experience, not because we have to. Or, maybe the robots will have taken over and we'll be working for them. *Who knows*?

My goal isn't to retire at sixty-five in the traditional sense, I enjoy my vocation and will be grateful if I can pursue writing in some way for as long as I'm able to. But I do want to reach a point where I can generate income on my terms. So, rather than worrying about not having enough money to leave the workforce with, I continue to reassess what life might look like through the lens of when I can depend less on a full-time salary, which involves building income-generating assets over time.

Couple goals check-in

No matter how far away retirement is for you, it might be worth having a chat with your partner about some of the financial realities that come with winding down your time in the workforce. Here are a couple of questions to get you started:

- What are our retirement lifestyle goals?
- Will we own our home by retirement?
- If we choose to rent into retirement, where will we live?
- How much superannuation do we need?
- How will we spend our days and what are the associated costs?

CHAPTER THIRTEEN

When the fairytale ends: divorce and separation

In the 2020-21 financial year, the Federal Circuit Court received 49,625 divorce applications, up 8 per cent on the previous year. This can perhaps be attributed to the pressure that Covid may have placed on already strained relationships, but that's a lot of people who needed to begin again, in just one year alone.

According to financial advisor Jess Brady, leaving relationships is often 'a difficult and often unsafe time, particularly for women'. If you are considering leaving a relationship, transparency and communication are great where appropriate, but sometimes a strategic exit is needed to keep you safe.

Jess says your first priority should be safety, then seeking legal counsel. But she adds that it can be wise to avoid an expensive legal battle because the money that is spent on legal proceedings is actually future money that could be invested in setting up a better life for yourself post-relationship.

We've spoken about binding financial agreements before, but these can be overridden when children are involved, so it pays to have all of your administration as up to date as possible prior to a separation. For example, you may have allocated something to a child when they were a dependent, but if they've since turned eighteen, they are no longer a financial dependent. Also make sure you check who your current superannuation beneficiary is and also check the status of any life insurance you hold. 'Insurance is a non-estate asset, if your ex-partner is the beneficiary and you pass away, they will automatically get that money and it can't be contested,' Jess cautions.

Whether you realise it at the time or not, you may go into survival mode upon exiting the relationship and simply be focused on pragmatic needs. People often end a partnership and move out, find a new place and start setting up a new life at lightning pace. Jess suggests that prior to purchasing new assets, give yourself enough time to adjust your headspace and think carefully about what you want your new life to look like.

CASE STUDY

Sebastian grew up in Adelaide, left school halfway through year twelve and began a pre-apprenticeship to become a chef. He met the woman who would become his wife at the age of twenty-one. Over time their relationship became more serious and after marrying, they sold their stuff and embarked on an adventure, travelling around Australia. Five months in, Sebastian's wife fell pregnant. 'We were in a van in Broome with zero assets or stability and decided this was no longer a good idea,' he says. 'I felt a sense of needing to look after the family unit and I was not set up financially for that at all.'

Their first daughter arrived when Sebastian was twenty-eight and when he turned thirty, their second daughter came along. Sebastian knew as the primary income earner that both the hours and the salary associated with life as a chef weren't sustainable for their growing family's needs and could prevent them from achieving their goal of owning a secure home.

In the early years of his children's life, the couple rented while Sebastian grew his career outside of the kitchen, first in catering and then in food service in the mining industry, during which time he made the sacrifice required to fly in and out of what became their hometown of Brisbane to save the funds to buy a house. It took until 2019 for the family to secure a historic Queenslander that they renovated. With a permanent address, they added two dogs to the family.

But soon after they achieved their dream, things began to unravel, and a separation ensued. The initial challenge was working out how to navigate a separation with two girls, a mortgage and two dogs. They remained in a cohabitation scenario for a few months. 'It took its toll, so I moved out,' Sebastian says.

At the beginning of the proceedings, Sebastian's lawyer told him going hard in a court battle could have cost him in excess of $50,000, so he sought to keep the financial dispute out of the courtroom.

When they began to discuss the division of assets, his lawyer recommended selling the property and splitting profits fairly, but Sebastian didn't want to do that – his primary reason wasn't money; it was his daughters. 'The girls have been dragged around the country. All they ever wanted was a home and two years after we bought one, it got blown apart. They need an anchor.'

Additionally, they are impressionable, and Sebastian knew, having seen his own parents go through a messy divorce, that he needed to set a better example than he'd witnessed during his own upbringing. 'They're two young women and I'm very conscious of my role in their lives. I'm their dad. I'll shape the way they have relationships.'

Sebastian first planned to buy his wife out and take the property at the market value, but his former partner instead decided she would buy him out. Even though her offer was below the market value, he accepted.

Why would he agree to this? Ultimately, he did it to move forward and as part of the agreement he's not required to pay ongoing maintenance for his teenage girls. 'Maintenance would be up to 40 per cent of my income,' he says.

He also kept all of his superannuation in the settlement. Plus, the home is in a good central location close to his work and the apartment he's renting. It means logistically life is reasonably seamless when it comes to picking up his daughters or taking them back to their mother.

'That process took ages because you can have all the conversations in the world, but you don't know someone until you divorce them. When shit gets real, people can lose track of their morals,' he says.

Today, Sebastian and his ex-wife have an itemised contract that covers what they're responsible for in terms of their girls' needs, right down to who pays for extracurricular lessons. Generally, they each cover costs when their daughters are with them and educational and other expenses are split in line with their incomes, meaning Sebastian pays about 64 per cent of each cost and his ex-wife pays the balance.

But even after the financial settlement, Sebastian still had a responsibility to his ex-wife until the divorce was finalised. 'If you don't lock in the divorce, you are responsible for the person. She could come back to me and say I've hurt myself at work and I would need to provide,' he says.

This period of limbo can become even more complex for people who meet someone else before the divorce is finalised, which was the case for Sebastian. His new partner Camille entered his life before Sebastian's divorce had been registered. In his case his first marriage was legally over soon after, but he warns people that proceedings can take years.

What are your options when you need to separate or divorce?

Family lawyer Pepe Kish says when a couple separates, the relationship isn't actually over yet, it's just changing, or going through the transition from being together to being separated. Until your property settlement is finalised, you will remain financially connected. And, if there are children involved, the relationship will continue in a co-parenting scenario, potentially for many years to come.

Kish believes, 'It's important to view it as a partnership and with any partnership it's better to be working together, rather than against one another.' We've all heard awful stories of nasty divorces that drag on for years where the hatred becomes entrenched and neither party really walks away happy. Before you embark on an expensive, anger-fuelled court battle, ask yourself if it is truly worth it. You might have heard of another case where a person got a 'good' outcome from going to court but that's rare, according to Pepe. Court is reserved for when two parties are often unwilling to come to an agreement. Do you really want to be those people? Court should be a last resort.

Ideally, people should have a clear understanding of their options 'while they're not in the throes of anxiety, distress, grief and anger'. Inevitably, though, most people don't know what to expect when they begin the process of separating or divorcing.

Kish uses the analogy of a staircase. 'At the end of your relationship you're at the bottom of the staircase. The top of the staircase is when the financial relationship has been severed and you're both free to commence your lives unencumbered. Along the staircase is a handrail that represents the law and associated legal advice. Most people are very capable of walking up a staircase and they know the handrail is there if they need to lean on it. It's especially useful if you're vulnerable.'

A vulnerable party might have taken a career break and therefore isn't earning income. They could also be a person suffering from an illness or someone whose primary role is to care for children.

Keeping proceedings out of court

You don't actually have to go to court to complete a financial settlement. Sadly, in dirty disputes that's where it can end up, but getting to that point is costly. Instead you might want to seek out one of the many alternatives that are available. Court really should be a last resort if you don't want to tip a small fortune into legal fees.

Mediation

Mediation is the most common form of alternative dispute resolution but the term is misleading because the word 'alternative' can create the sense that it is not the primary means to resolve matters when in fact it could be far less painful than court proceedings. Mediation is 'without prejudice dispute resolution', which means that during mediation you're able to have a free and open discussion and whatever you say can't be held against you in court in the event that you do end up there.

Basically, it's a chance to bring your ideas for settlement to the table but you won't be held to any proposals you make.

In the case of mediation, a qualified, independent and neutral person will facilitate the process which could take just a few hours if it's straightforward but longer if it's complex or you're struggling to reach an agreement. Mediation can occur between you, your partner and the mediator only, or with lawyers assisting.

Collaborative law

Perhaps you don't want to go to court, but you and your former partner both want lawyers involved in your settlement. In such a scenario, collaborative law could be a good option. This is a process in which your lawyers – instead of acting as adversaries – sit with you to resolve matters. You also sign a contract agreeing not to go to court.

In collaborative law, often a multi-disciplinary approach is needed and other people such as financial professionals and therapists can assist to help parties reach an agreement.

Pepe reflects, 'No-fault divorce is wonderful because you're not blaming the other person – but one downside is if you feel wronged at law that's considered irrelevant. We know that's not irrelevant when you're going through it. The collaborative law space allows those feelings to be explored.'

In collaborative law, the fees can generally be approximately $20,000, but if you have a dispute that you're not able to resolve through negotiation, it could be an excellent way to make progress with a holistic view of the issue, rather than simply focusing on who gets what.

Arbitration

Family law arbitration is a process where a neutral third party, called an arbitrator, helps resolve financial disputes related to family matters. It cannot be utilised to resolve things such as parenting disputes, it can only be used for financial matters. The arbitrator will listen to both sides, consider evidence and make a binding decision, known as an award, which is filed at court and becomes the binding order that the parties must follow. Arbitration provides a more private, cost effective and flexible alternative to going to court.

As a guide, you can expect arbitration to cost somewhere between $20,000 and $30,000, but there can be many variables. Costs can come in at more when things such as property valuations and other administrative costs are factored in. Still, it's likely to be far less expensive than a full court procedure.

Private agreement

Finally, in a de facto separation that doesn't require a divorce, you can make a private agreement and not involve the law at all. But most family law specialists would strongly encourage people to seek their own legal advice to make sure they're aware of their options and any risks or benefits. Consider state and territory-based situations such as the transfer of property. In the ACT, for example, if you're transferring property you can apply for a stamp-duty exemption on the transfer. In addition, if you sell a property, you can use the proceeds of the sale and claim the stamp-duty exemption on your new home. That's not the case in every state, but the point is that there could be significant financial implications long after a separation. Additionally, if you agree to split superannuation, you can't do that without a binding financial agreement or order of the court in place.

A private agreement might feel like the most financially viable way to navigate a split in the moment, but there's a period of time where the parties are able to come back for 'another bite of the cherry'. Say, for example, you move on and buy a house, your ex-partner may wonder where you got the money to do that and make a claim on it.

'Anything that you may informally agree on won't be considered binding or enforceable in any way. You will not be able to enforce your ex to comply with any terms you agreed to informally,' Pepe explains.

If you want to protect your private agreement with legally binding parameters, you can apply for a consent order and formalise it under the law. A consent order makes any agreement you have reached legally binding. Generally, consent orders made by court are either parenting orders or financial orders. They should be filed within a year of a divorce or within two years of the end of a de facto partnership.

As difficult as it might be to formalise your agreement when ending your relationship even when it is truly amicable, delaying a financial settlement may have significant ramifications.

Avoiding court

Not only is court a last resort due to the emotional toll it takes, it's also a massive financial hit, with litigated matters that proceed all the way to a final hearing potentially costing each individual up to $150,000, or more if you engage the top lawyers and take the matter all the way to a final hearing. For more information about the court hearing types, visit the Federal Circuit and Family Court of Australia website (fcfcoa.gov.au).

CASE STUDY

Queensland-based Charlotte, forty-four, was with her husband Peter for seventeen years before they separated. They remained separated for four years before they divorced.

Peter first moved into a friend's place. He was chronically ill, and because they were separated, he was now eligible for the disability pension, meaning Charlotte no longer had to support him financially, which she'd been doing for some time.

'There was an idea we'd still try to get back together if he got counselling, so we didn't 100 per cent say it was over for another eighteen months. And then life was busy – there were no arguments, no reason to hurry (so I thought) and so we didn't prioritise the divorce,' she says.

It wasn't until Charlotte found out that financial splits didn't take effect from separation, and she started to worry that he could be entitled to a share of the business she was building. Although she was less concerned about her ex who was 'at heart, a decent person'. Rather she explains, 'Because he was chronically ill, there was a possibility that if his health deteriorated, a new partner or someone representing him could make a claim.'

In delaying their financial settlement, there were risks for both Charlotte and Peter. 'If he or I had inherited money in a will or received a compensation payout before the financial settlement was finalised, the other party could have been entitled to half,' Charlotte says.

Charlotte has a law degree and says that despite her education she was 'absolutely clueless about the legalities of separation and divorce'. Before she engaged a lawyer, she struggled to get answers about the exact point that the assets would be split, which was important as her business was gaining momentum. 'Once we actually applied for divorce by mutual consent, I discovered the financial assets needed to be finalised within twelve months, and that assets would be calculated at the time of the financial settlement.' Meaning, her growing business could be worth more in twelve months time, which could in turn impact the division of assets. In short: the sooner Charlotte had this resolved, the better.

Charlotte and Peter had to finesse their numbers to best reflect what they wanted to happen. Rather than fight over who got what percentage of the house, they agreed that, 'I would buy Peter out from his half of the house, but we would each keep what we had, including our roughly similar superannuation,' Charlotte says.

But Charlotte points out that even an amicable agreement must be deemed fair and reasonable if you want your consent order approved. Because Peter was unwell, it could have been possible for the courts to give more weight to that. In other words, Peter could have been entitled to a share of the business or a bigger share of the house. 'From the court's perspective, even though I was earning just a tiny income from my small startup, I was still "a business owner", while my ex was on the disability pension with no likely prospects to earn his own salary again.'

Charlotte had also spent the four years they were separated living in her parents' granny flat and saving every cent she could to try to buy the house, whereas her ex had been getting himself into debt. That meant when they came to the settlement, all those years of Charlotte being responsible made the financial position between them look even more unbalanced. There was far more nuance than that, but the court doesn't always make decisions based on nuance.

Charlotte had a friend in a similar position, whose first consent order was rejected by the court. Her ex-husband was also on a disability pension after churning through a significant payout from his former employer. Because he'd spent it before the financial settlement and was broke again, his ex-wife had to pay him more of a share for the house to get it through the courts.

'In the end, our consent order was approved,' Charlotte says. She secured a mortgage to buy Peter out of the house. 'One thing we had to promise the court was that he would be allowed to remain a tenant in the house for at least three years and would get lower-than-market-rate rent for that time,' she says. She's allowed to put it up during that time, but it must always remain at least 15 per cent lower than the market rate.

It was an outcome that she was happy with as long as her small business, and therefore her future livelihood, was protected.

'If he had been the kind of person to try to take a share of my business on an ongoing basis, I would have probably had to look at closing it down and starting from scratch,' Charlotte says. 'In hindsight, what I wish I had done was consult a family lawyer when we agreed the split was final to get my facts straight and started working on the financial settlement early. Even if I wasn't in a position to buy the house from him earlier, we might have had an agreement in place, so that any assets or debts in the intervening years would not have been affected.'

Couple goals check-in

No one wants to talk about the possible end of the relationship but far from being taboo, a transparent conversation about a potential split is a reasonable and healthy idea. Here are some subjects you might want to broach with your partner:

- What would happen to our assets in the event of a split?
- Do we need to formalise any of our current verbal agreements?
- How would a separation impact our children if we have them?
- If we did separate or divorce, how could we minimise the legal costs and manage the process as amicably as possible?

CHAPTER FOURTEEN

Future-proofing your couple goals

By June 2023, Sam and I had recovered from our wedding, started some minor renovations in our kitchen and finished working with financial planner Rebecca Pritchard to finalise our long-term money strategy. Ultimately, we now have all of our income going into one account known as our 'cash hub'. We made this decision under Rebecca's guidance because it means we have one central platform that enables us to keep track of where our money is going.

This creates shared accountability and transparency – it's also seamless. From this fund we pay our mortgage and all of our big expenses: car repayments, utilities and so on. We don't need to have discussions about who owes what on a given bill or whether we're putting enough towards a goal because it's entirely automated, based on our cashflow. We don't fixate on who earns what or whether we're appropriately splitting costs, which in turn is great for our relationship. Income doesn't necessarily reflect how challenging your job is. Whether you're a teacher, cleaner, healthcare worker, tradesperson, hospitality employee, home-based primary carer, entrepreneur or accountant, you probably need to push your brain, your body, or both. So tying a monetary value to your relationship dynamic can be unfair and erode both equality and intimacy over time. The largely shared approach Sam and I have chosen is right for us as an established couple with shared long-term financial responsibilities and objectives, but it took time to get here.

I will admit this was a psychological transition for both of us. We've both been financially independent throughout our working lives, but in our circumstances, the case for pooling most of our income was compelling. It stacked up from the admin, mental load and transparency perspective; and the financial projections for our future look significantly better using a shared cashflow and surplus deployment than they would if we'd continued to run our money management separately.

Although all of our income goes to one shared account, a portion is then redirected to our personal accounts each week so that we can save or spend our individual cut freely. As we've discussed in early chapters, having your own personal account is good for your autonomy, and allows you to avoid being entirely financially enmeshed. When we went through this process, we both ensured we maintained our own accounts, which we then top up each week. These are accounts we had prior to meeting, in our names only. I can't access Sam's and he can't access mine. If either of us want to buy new clothes or go out with our mates, we don't argue about how much was spent.

Our couple goals

The remaining amount of money we have each month, after household expenses and personal spending, is surplus income that is allocated across our shared goals, so our strategy looks something like the diagram on the next page.

I say something like this because we set up our cash hub with the view to disburse portions of our surplus to each of the goals I've highlighted, but there was also room to move if our cashflow wasn't so … flowy. In a high inflation economy, that was entirely possible, so our goal disbursements were established to ensure they could be switched on and off or dialled up and down at any time if our circumstances required. In simple terms, these are direct transfers to each of our goal accounts. We can pause them, increase and reduce the amounts we're contributing to our goals. In particular, when we've finished our renovation, we can redirect surplus funds to existing goals or set new ones.

As you can see, each of our goals has a 'why' and a few values tied to it. This means they're underpinned by who we are as individuals and where we want to go as a couple.

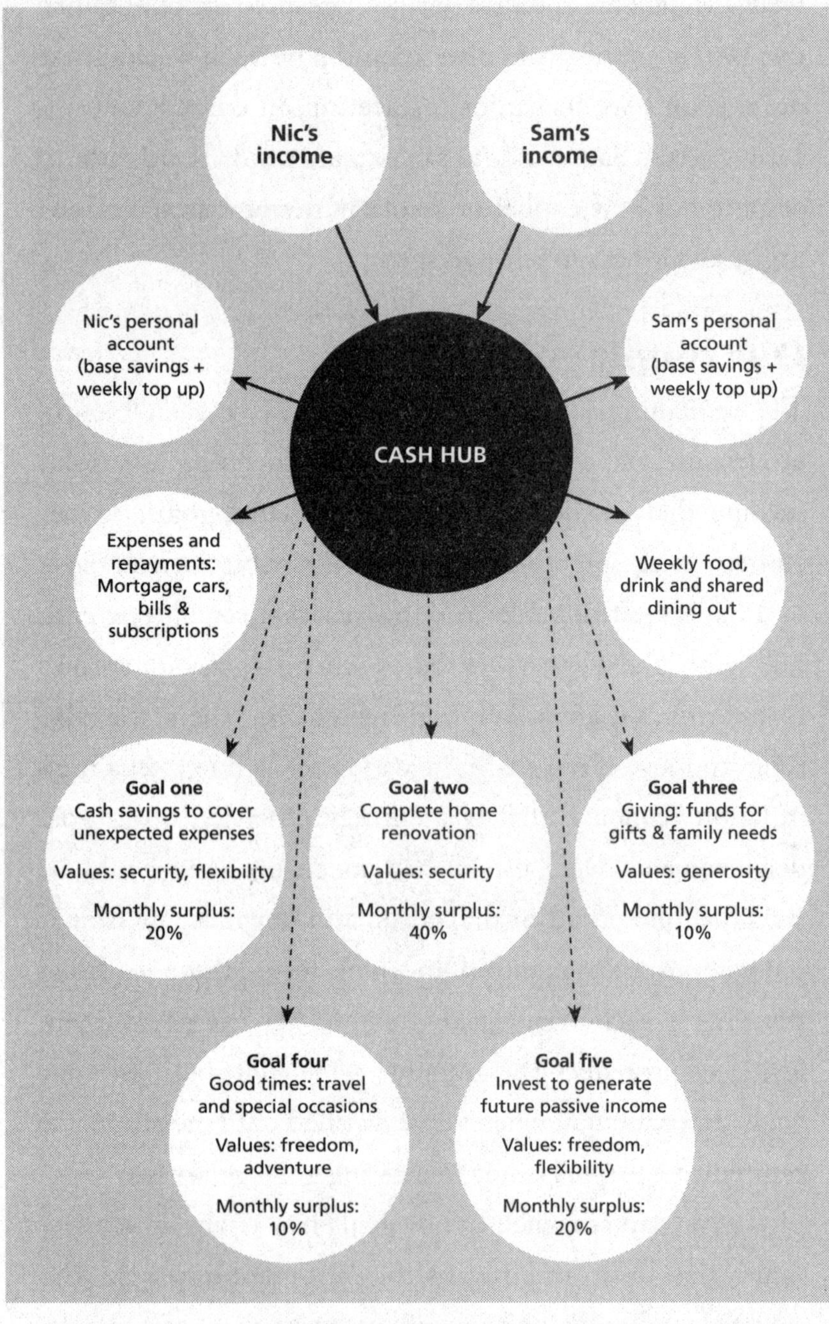
Nic's income
Sam's income
Nic's personal account (base savings + weekly top up)
CASH HUB
Sam's personal account (base savings + weekly top up)
Expenses and repayments: Mortgage, cars, bills & subscriptions
Weekly food, drink and shared dining out
Goal one
Cash savings to cover unexpected expenses
Values: security, flexibility
Monthly surplus: 20%
Goal two
Complete home renovation
Values: security
Monthly surplus: 40%
Goal three
Giving: funds for gifts & family needs
Values: generosity
Monthly surplus: 10%
Goal four
Good times: travel and special occasions
Values: freedom, adventure
Monthly surplus: 10%
Goal five
Invest to generate future passive income
Values: freedom, flexibility
Monthly surplus: 20%

If we were doing these things simply to build wealth, without a motivation, there'd be a risk of us finding excuses to spend elsewhere. The position we've landed in is the result of regular chats about which of our values to prioritise now. This in turn dictates the percentage of the surplus that goes to each goal.

As we tick things off, we'll reassess which goals and values deserve more attention and alter the surplus split as needed. That's why our home and cash savings are getting the bulk of the surplus right now. These goals help us to build security, which is the foundation for future goals. Getting this right will hopefully give us more flexibility in time. When we've made more headway, we'll be able to give our values of freedom, adventure and generosity some extra love. While all of our big goals are shared for now, the flexibility we're setting up will make space for personal pursuits in the future.

A note on our financial planning experience

When I started writing this book, I intended to interview financial planners and advisors. Even I struggled with the concept of spending thousands on a tailored financial plan. But what began as an interview with Rebecca did become full-blown financial advice. That's because our early conversations helped me to see that the upfront spend could quickly be offset by more effective money management. It has been invaluable, because Sam and I met and married within a year, so we hadn't enjoyed the benefits of working out how to manage money together over an extended period. We had a *lot* of financial administration to work through, and in the financial advice process we found a one-stop shop for sorting out our financial life admin. Having Rebecca to guide us through everything from insurance to superannuation was worth every cent. In fact, seeing a complete picture of our present financial situation and where it could take us made us think far more critically about where we were putting our money. One of our big goals during our early discussions had been a significant kitchen renovation but doing that would prevent us from having other things. So, in the end, we did the minor kitchen upgrade ourselves and allocated what would have been spent on that project elsewhere.

That said, financial planning is not the most fun way to spend thousands of dollars. We started the process in early 2023 and it took months to transition our accounts to a shared system. But part of the reason is that we really dragged our feet at times because we both resented the administration when we had so many other obligations. Financial planners don't just wave a magic wand and instantly recalibrate your accounts. There's a lot of set-up work on your end, too. We did this while simultaneously planning a wedding and renovating a house, and in hindsight we reckon we would have waited a touch longer until we could give it the mental energy it deserved.

But then again, there's always an excuse if you allow it, so we're glad we pushed through. It's much easier once the strategy is in place and foundation has been laid, though.

In terms of cost, I was surprised to learn that we could pay a chunk of our fees from our superannuation funds. We also didn't pay for the service until after we had our statement of advice, about three months in. The statement of advice is the document that outlines all of the recommendations based on the information you've provided to the financial planner. You may be able to negotiate your payment terms depending on your circumstances. At the time, the initial financial advice fee was not tax deductible, but subsequent ongoing fees would qualify as a tax deduction. Finally, for us, we believe the cost of the service and advice will be cancelled out by running a cashflow that generates a surplus, along with the growth in superannuation and investment products we've been exposed to. The high-quality insurance we have in place in the event anything goes wrong also provides invaluable peace of mind.

A good financial planner will create fee options that suit you and your needs depending on where you're at in life. One of my concerns had been getting 'locked in' and paying advice fees indefinitely. In our case, we paid to have the strategy set up, and for support in the implementation, then committed to an 'unstructured' approach to our planning needs, meaning we don't pay for full service annually. Now that we have a strategy, we can execute it ourselves.

This may change as our circumstances evolve, but it works for us at this point in time.

Your couple goals

Financially, and personally, your goals will of course look different to ours, but I hope you've used the conversation starters throughout this book to get clearer about your individual and shared aspirations. Ideally, the expert guidance provided by the psychologists, lawyers and financial planners has helped you to see the value in talking about your shared financial future.

You may decide that maintaining financial autonomy or splitting your costs as a percentage based on your income is best for you. It will probably depend on the stage you're in. What's important is that you both wholeheartedly agree with your approach, and that you communicate regularly. I'd argue that your biggest chance of achieving your goals isn't based on how much you earn or how wild your dream is, it's how well you talk about it. And, further to that, how far in advance you start talking about it. If, for example, the goal is based on a significant life milestone such as buying a house, having children, or even retiring, your strongest tools are communication coupled with time. Having adequate time to prepare to meet your target will likely make the process far less stressful. If you can, speak with a licensed professional who can help you to take a holistic look at your present position and help you to build a strategy.

The ultimate couple goals

By now, you're hopefully really clear on what it takes to achieve your couple goals, but I've saved a pretty important piece of information until last: your ability to convert goals to real outcomes relies heavily on your relationship being healthy and secure. That doesn't mean you won't face conflict or have periods of difficulty, but you do genuinely need to be good for one another if you're going to go the distance.

Research indicates that happily married and long-term de facto couples are less likely to experience chronic disease than singles, but the key word there is *happily*. I was always of the view that I'd rather be on my own than be in an unfulfilling relationship.

I'm grateful to have found a man who is an equal. He makes an exceptional slow-cooked beef brisket and is the superior bathroom cleaner. Even when we're watching our spending, we make a point of having fun. Life is serious, there's lots of serious stuff in this book, so I want to leave you with a reminder to play, too.

In light and playful moments, I forget about the mortgage, work and retirement-savings targets. I'm prone to overthinking and worrying into the future, and Sam always knows when and how to unravel me.

We've had our fair share of magical days and completely shit days. We've drawn on the guidance from the experts consulted for this book on countless occasions.

We also have lots of small goals that don't cost us anything. Sam's currently teaching me how to play the guitar. In terms of personal goals, I intend to get more involved in our community and expand my regional relationships, while Sam would like to write more of his own music.

But I also know there are difficult times to come. This is inevitable, so I asked a range of people in long-term relationships what they do to keep their relationships fulfilling, loving and thriving. As far as I'm concerned, anyone who's still happily together ten, twenty, thirty, forty or more years later is the final word in couple goals. Most of their tips aren't explicitly financial, it's always going to be your shared values and commitment that help you to achieve your monetary targets. Being rich in these tools is what makes any couple truly wealthy.

You have to make space for the unexpected, and that's the case for Kath, who met her husband twenty-five years ago. They were engaged within three months and married fifteen months later. He now has a neurological disorder that affects his cognitive function and also causes seizures and chronic pain. Kath says, 'For better or worse really applies. You have to be there for each other, no matter what.'

Another key to long-term success is accepting that you and your partner will have different histories, hang-ups and habits, says Brooke, who's been in a relationship for twenty years. In her case, that meant bringing some 'less-than-great' money habits to the relationship, which have affected their shared finances. They have worked to prioritise 'accountability without judgement' and create a safe space for honesty about spending. 'It gives me freedom to know he expects honesty from me, but also understands we're both just humans doing the best we can,' she says.

After more than seventeen years together, Kristy and Karina have been tremendously happy, saying their secret is to 'never stop dating or surprising each other'.

Linley has just celebrated thirty years with her husband and tells me the key to their enduring love is 'unwavering support, trust and loads of laughs' along the way.

Finally, there is John and Franki, who met in 1981 and have raised three children and navigated the course of life together for more than forty years. They say, 'You always have to put your heads together and plan for the future. Then, keep talking about your plan as life changes.' John adds that when they're thrown a curveball, their secret is to 'always re-evaluate and count our blessings when life is rough'.

ENDNOTES

CHAPTER ONE

P.20, Australia has a very – Wade, M., 'The male breadwinner is an outdated relic', *Sydney Morning Herald*, 27 July 2016. smh.com.au/opinion/the-male-breadwinner-is-an-outdated-relic-20160726-gqdzo4.html

P. 22, In 2022, the national – 'Equal Day Pay 2022', Workplace Gender Equality Agency, 2022. wgea.gov.au/gender-pay-gap-data/equal-pay-day-2022

P. 22, A 2023 article from – Humphery-Jenner, M., 'Australia's new pay equality law risks failing women – unless we make this simple fix', *The Conversation*, 10 February 2023. theconversation.com/australias-new-pay-equality-law-risks-failing-women-unless-we-make-this-simple-fix-199587

P. 23, According to the 2021 – 'The ABS data gender pay gap', Workplace Gender Equality Agency, 2023. wgea.gov.au/data-statistics/ABS-gender-pay-gap-data

P. 23, Although women required a – Foster, E., 'Women holding keys to the housing market', *Westpac*, 5 February 2018. westpac.com.au/news/money-matters/2018/02/women-holding-the-keys-to-the-housing-market/

P. 24, Statistically speaking, he probably – 'Stay-at-home dads: Still rare but numbers rising', Australian Institute of Family Studies, 5 April 2018. aifs.gov.au/sites/default/files/stay_at_home_dads-media_release_0_0_0.pdf

P. 25, And yet the Australian – Bahar, E. et al., 'Children and the gender earnings gap: Evidence for Australia', The Australian Government The Treasury, March 2023. treasury.gov.au/sites/default/files/2023-03/p2023-372004.pdf

CHAPTER THREE

P. 47, The results of a – research conducted by Jessica Brady with market research company YouGov, a nationally representative sample of 1,023 Australians aged 18 yrs+, 2023

P. 48, According to behavioural scientist – Interview with Lucille Shackleton, 15 November 2022

P. 48, Therapist McKimmie says couples – Interview with Isiah McKimmie, 31 October 2022

P. 48, Research from the Gottman – Interview with Lucille Shackleton, 15 November 2022

CHAPTER FOUR

P. 69, According to a 2022 – 'The cost of financial abuse in Australia', Commonwealth Bank and Deloitte Access Economics report, 2022. commbank.com.au/content/dam/caas/newsroom/docs/Cost%20of%20financial%20abuse%20in%20Australia.pdf

P. 70, According to the Australian – Wright, S., 'When women earn more than their male partners, domestic violence risk goes up 35 per cent', *Sydney Morning Herald*, 30 March 2021. smh.com.au/politics/federal/when-women-earn-more-than-their-male-partners-domestic-violence-risk-goes-up-35-per-cent-20210329-p57cwb.html

P. 70, Forensic accountant Suzanne Delbridge – Interview with Suzanne Delbridge, 15 February 2023

P. 74, A 2022 study out of – Gladstone J.J., Garbinsky E.N. and Mogilner, C., 'Pooling Finances and Relationship Satisfaction', *Journal of Personality and Social Psychology*, Cornell University, 2022

P. 84, Your relationship status will – Interview with Julian Mauro, 11 November 2022

CHAPTER FIVE

P. 93, When we think about – 'What is the Sound Relationship House?' The Gottman Institute. gottman.com/blog/what-is-the-sound-relationship-house/ and Interview with Lucille Shackleton, 15 November 2022

CHAPTER SEVEN

P. 134, There are more than – 'SMEs are the lifeblood of the Australian Economy', Australian Banking Association, 2022. ausbanking.org.au/wp-content/uploads/2022/11/ABA-SME-Lending-Report-2022.pdf

P. 153, Research from the Australian – Interview with Talya Faigenbaum, principal family lawyer at Nest Legal, the Australian Institute of Family Studies (AIFS), 9 February 2023

CHAPTER EIGHT

P. 170, According to accountant Julian – Interview with Julian Mauro, 11 November 2022

P. 172, But it's worth nothing – Hendy, N., 'Bank of Mum and Dad a rich source for first-home deposit', *Australian Financial Review*, 2 March 2022. afr.com/wealth/investing/bank-of-mum-and-dad-a-rich-source-for-first-home-deposit-20220223-p59ytj

CHAPTER NINE

P. 185, According to the Bureau – 'Marriages and divorces, Australia: National and state statistics on marriages and divorces, including same-sex couples, presented by age, duration and rates', Australian Bureau of Statistics, 10 November 2022. abs.gov.au/statistics/people/people-and-communities/marriages-and-divorces-australia/latest-release

P. 186, Bridal stores in Australia – 'Bridal Stores – Market Size (2008–2030)', IBISWorld, 3 October 2023. ibisworld.com/au/market-size/bridal-stores/

P. 188, Well, according to research – 'Getting married', ASIC consumer website. moneysmart.gov.au/family-and-relationships/getting-married

P. 188, Financial advisor Jess Brady – Interview with Jessica Brady, 15 November 2022

P. 189, One study suggests that – Xiao, J.J.; Porto, N., 'Present bias and financial behaviour', *Human Development and Family Science*, Faculty Publications, University of Rhode Island, 2019. digitalcommons.uri.edu/hdf_facpubs/67/

CHAPTER TEN

P. 199, In 2020, one in – Aubusson, K., 'One in 18 babies conceived by IVF but success can depend on choice of clinic', *Sydney Morning Herald*, 16 October 2022. smh.com.au/national/one-in-18-babies-conceived-by-ivf-but-success-can-depend-on-choice-of-clinic-20221014-p5bpwd.html

P. 203, The 85-page national strategy – 'Women's Budget Statement October 2022–23', *The Commonwealth of Australia*, October 2023. archive.budget.gov.au/2022-23-october/womens-statement/download/womens_budget_statement_2022-23.pdf

P. 203, The strategy 'outlines a – ibid

P. 204, Federal treasury research indicates – Bahar, E. et al., 'Children and the gender earnings gap', The Australian Government Treasury, October 2022. treasury.gov.au/sites/default/files/2022-11/p2022-325290-children.pdf

P. 206, Parental Leave Pay is – 'How much you can get', Services Australia, July 2023. servicesaustralia.gov.au/how-much-parental-leave-pay-you-can-get-for-child-born-or-adopted-from-1-july-2023?context=64479

P. 207, A recent survey by – 'ASFA calls on Government to close retirement savings gender gap', Association of Superannuation Funds of Australia, 7 March 2023. superannuation.asn.au/media/media-releases/2023/media-release-7-march-2023

P. 208, 'Financial planning associated with children' – Interview with Jessica Brady, 15 November 2022

P. 208, Financial planner Rebecca Pritchard – Interview with Rebecca Pritchard, 1 February 2023

P. 215, Those with best practice offerings – Black, E., 'These companies have the best parental leave perks', *Australian Financial Review*, 17 October 2022. afr.com/work-and-careers/workplace/these-companies-have-the-best-parental-leave-perks-20220926-p5bkzd

P. 215, Over at EnergyAustralia – Topsfield, J., 'Part-time pay, full-time super: How one company aims to close to gap', *The Age*, 8 June 2022. theage.com.au/business/companies/part-time-pay-full-time-super-how-one-company-aims-to-close-the-gap-20220608-p5as32.html

P. 217, According to research, during – 'What to Expect (Finally) When You're Expecting', Canstar, 2021. ogcg.com.au/wp-content/uploads/2022/01/What-to-Expect-Financially-When-You-Are-Expecting.pdf

CHAPTER ELEVEN

P. 228, I was stunned to – Eyers, J., 'Heavenly service: Start-up raises for "end-of-life" digital platform', *Australian Financial Review*, 18 October 2021.afr.com/technology/heavenly-service-start-up-raises-for-end-of-life-digital-platform-20211014-p5904s

P. 229, However, legal experts say – Interview with Adam Lubovsky, Safewill, 16 November 2022

P. 235, Also – this might sound – Interview with Laura Vickers, 9 February 2023

P. 240, But according to the – ibid

CHAPTER TWELVE

P. 254, The foundations of the – Cooley, P.L., Hubbard, C.M. and Walz, D.T., 'Retirement savings: Choosing a withdrawal rate that is sustainable', February 1998. aaii.com/files/pdf/6794_retirement-savings-choosing-a-withdrawal-rate-that-is-sustainable.pdf

P. 263, According to the *Australian Financial Review* – Dean, L., 'Nearly 300,000 people, (mostly Millennials) became traders last year', *Australian Financial Review*, 3 March 2022. afr.com/wealth/investing/nearly-300-000-mostly-millennials-became-traders-last-year-20220302-p5a151

P. 269, In the early 1990s – 'Life tables: Statistics about life tables for Australia, states and territories and life expectancy at birth estimates for sub-state regions', Australian Bureau of Statistics, 8 November 2022. abs.gov.au/statistics/people/population/life-tables/latest-release

CHAPTER THIRTEEN

P. 273, In the 2020–21 financial – '2020-21 Federal Circuit Court Annual Report', Federal Circuit and Family Court of Australia, 2021. fcfcoa.gov.au/fcc-annual-reports/2020-21/part-3

CHAPTER FOURTEEN

P. 299, Research indicates that happily – Devlin, H., 'In sickness and in health? Signs couples live longer shouldn't worry singletons', *The Guardian*, 4 March 2023. theguardian.com/society/2023/mar/03/in-sickness-and-health-signs-couples-live-longer-shouldnt-worry-singletons

ACKNOWLEDGEMENTS

The initial idea for this book surfaced just months into my relationship with Sam. When I asked him how he felt about me writing about our personal and financial life, he immediately gave me his full support. Thank you, Sam, for wholeheartedly encouraging me to pursue my goals; I will always do the same for you.

To my agent, Alex Adsett, you've been with me for three books now and your commitment to getting them out into the world is a magical balance of sunshine and tenacity. I'm eternally grateful for your passion, happy face and hard work.

My publisher, Scott Henderson, I love the way you didn't even try to play it cool when you read my first pages. Thank you for seeing the potential and understanding how valuable this book could be for couples who want to work more effectively as a team. Your collaborative nature has been an absolute gift; I'm so fortunate to have your backing.

Massive thanks to my editor Jacquie Brown and also Samantha Sainsbury and the Hachette editorial team. Your attention to detail and dedication to making *Couple Goals* great has been outstanding. I know how many people touched these pages in the process and it's better for each contribution.

To the Hachette marketing and publicity team, particularly Cosima Toni, I'm stoked to have you playing the important role of awareness across digital and mainstream media. Thank you so much for your creativity and enthusiasm.

Many experts shared an incredible amount of time and knowledge with me because they understand how important it is for couples to harness the power of good financial management and life admin. Thanks in particular to Rebecca Pritchard and the team at Rising Tide Financial (risingtidefinancial.com.au) for nudging us into financial shape and enhancing our relationship in the process.

Thanks also to Jessica Brady (jessicabrady.com.au), Laura Vickers (nestlegal.com.au), Julian Mauro (mauro.net.au) and Pepe Kish (balancefamilylaw.com.au), who went over and above to make sure the information I shared was accurate, and thank you to my case study interviewees, who kindly told me their stories.

A shout out to my readers. I know some of you have been following along since *Smashed Avo*, thank you. This book is not just for people in relationships right now and I'm glad you've read it regardless of the phase you're in. Life is a wild ride, and I believe the more financial literacy you have, the better equipped you are to handle the bumpy bits.

Finally, to our loved ones: Mum, Dad, Dan and the Kalken clan, Kate, Paul, Joel, Christine, Brydie, Zack, Michaela, Saskia, Margot, Matt, Beck, Jimmy, Sally, David, Chris, Jake and the many others who surround us, you're all bloody wonderful.

hachette
AUSTRALIA

If you would like to find out more about Hachette Australia, our authors, upcoming events and new releases, you can visit our website or our social media channels:

hachette.com.au

HachetteAustralia

HachetteAus